EPIC

This student guidebook offers a clear introduction to an often complex and unwieldy area of literary studies. Tracing epic from its ancient and classical roots through post-modern and contemporary examples this volume discusses:

- a wide range of writers including Homer, Virgil, Ovid, Dante, Chaucer, Milton, Cervantes, Keats, Byron, Eliot, Walcott and Tolkien
- texts from poems, novels, children's literature, television, theatre and film
- themes and motifs such as romance, tragedy, religion, journeys and the supernatural.

Offering new directions for the future and addressing the place of epic in both English-language texts and World Literature, this handy book takes you on a fascinating guided tour through the epic.

Paul Innes is a senior lecturer at the University of Glasgow. He has published widely on Shakespeare, early modern literature and literary theory.

THE NEW CRITICAL IDIOM

SERIES EDITOR: JOHN DRAKAKIS, UNIVERSITY OF STIRLING

The New Critical Idiom is an invaluable series of introductory guides to today's critical terminology. Each book:

- provides a handy, explanatory guide to the use (and abuse) of the term;
- offers an original and distinctive overview by a leading literary and cultural critic;
- relates the term to the larger field of cultural representation.

With a strong emphasis on clarity, lively debate and the widest possible breadth of examples, *The New Critical Idiom* is an indispensable approach to key topics in literary studies.

Also available in this series:

EPIC

Paul Innes

Routledge
Taylor & Francis Group

LONDON AND NEW YORK

First published 2013
by Routledge
2 Park Square, Milton Park, Abingdon, Oxon OX14 4RN

Simultaneously published in the USA and Canada
by Routledge
711 Third Avenue, New York, NY 10017

Routledge is an imprint of the Taylor & Francis Group, an informa business

British Library Cataloguing in Publication Data
A catalogue record for this book is available from the British Library

Library of Congress Cataloging in Publication Data
Innes, Paul, 1964–
Epic / Paul Innes.
p. cm. – (The new critical idiom)
Includes bibliographical references and index.
1. Epic literature – History and criticism.
2. Epic films – History and criticism. I. Title.
PN56.E65I56 2013
809'.9357 – dc23   2012033101

ISBN: 978-0-415-58738-9 (hbk)
ISBN: 978-0-415-58739-6 (pbk)
ISBN: 978-0-203-14825-9 (ebk)

Typeset in Garamond
by Taylor & Francis Books

MIX
Paper from
responsible sources
FSC
www.fsc.org   FSC® C004839   Printed and bound in Great Britain by the MPG Books Group

CONTENTS

SERIES EDITOR'S PREFACE

The New Critical Idiom is a series of introductory books which seeks to extend the lexicon of literary terms, in order to address the radical changes which have taken place in the study of literature during the last decades of the twentieth century. The aim is to provide clear, well-illustrated accounts of the full range of terminology currently in use, and to evolve histories of its changing usage.

The current state of the discipline of literary studies is one where there is considerable debate concerning basic questions of terminology. This involves, among other things, the boundaries which distinguish the literary from the non-literary; the position of literature within the larger sphere of culture; the relationship between literatures of different cultures; and questions concerning the relation of literary to other cultural forms within the context of interdisciplinary studies.

It is clear that the field of literary criticism and theory is a dynamic and heterogeneous one. The present need is for individual volumes on terms which combine clarity of exposition with an adventurousness of perspective and a breadth of application. Each volume will contain as part of its apparatus some indication of the direction in which the definition of particular terms is likely to move, as well as expanding the disciplinary boundaries within which some of these terms have been traditionally contained. This will involve some re-situation of terms within the larger field of cultural representation, and will introduce examples from the area of film and the modern media in addition to examples from a variety of literary texts.

ACKNOWLEDGEMENTS

Many thanks are due to Emma Joyes and Niall Slater at Routledge for their unfailing editorial support and their under-standing of academics and their foibles. However, my main thanks go to my wife, Cathy, and her even greater ability to put up with me in particular. This book is dedicated to her.

1

EPIC LITERARY HISTORY

Epic was once considered to be the highest literary form, a poet's greatest achievement. Its cultural importance was such that entire societies could be defined by and through it. Ancient Greece produced Homer's *Iliad* and *Odyssey*; Rome had Virgil and the *Aeneid*. In the Judaeo-Christian tradition, the first five books of the Old Testament could be considered to be an epic. Later books that deal with the establishment of the Kingdoms of Judea and Israel could additionally be defined as variants of historical epic. The Bible differs from the classical Western lineage in not being consciously poetic and in not being supposedly written by one person, but the two traditions have one major defining feature in common: status. The epic in this view is an identifiable literary form with a crucial cultural prominence. Its scope lends itself to grand narratives that incorporate various myths of origin intermingled with memories of historical events and personages. It passes through various stages, with particularly critical resonance for English poetry as it accompanies the development of a nascent British Empire. Spenser and Milton both, in their own ways, seed their work with a peculiarly Protestant epic *ethos*. Recent modern writing such as Walcott's *Omeros* and

Atwood's *Penelopiad* revisit this long history through their respective post-colonial and feminist intertextual retrospectives.

However, it should not be forgotten that the epic developed out of a communal impetus to cultural memory before it became a written form. The verbal and performative elements play off against the literary in different ways for different cultures, and therefore historical precision needs to be applied to individual epic texts in order to avoid generalisation. For example, the *Aeneid* is conceived and executed as a purely literary form, one that is engaged in conversation with its Homeric predecessors, in addition to other considerations. It is not produced by and for an oral/aural community in and through performance. Even so, much of its reworking of the myths of Roman origins is derived from folk traditions. Many more examples could be adduced of the ways in which different epics work through the relationship between the oral and the literary, something that is a main concern of the present volume. Jack Goody points to the inherent difficulties in unravelling how epic relates to the society that produces it, especially when that society is almost entirely non-literate. His chapter on Africa, Greece and oral poetry in *The Interface Between the Written and the Oral* (Goody 1993: 78–109) is of particular value in relation to this issue. He characterises the processes of composition and performance of oral African works and he then uses these as a point of departure, producing a comparative methodology by which he is able to draw analogies with Homer's Greek-speaking culture. Goody's point is that there is no straightforward or clear-cut distinction between a purely oral culture and its epics on the one hand, and a purely literate one on the other. Instead, there is a series of possible combinations between the two extremes.

It is tempting to articulate the relationship between the oral and the literate in terms of a classic binary opposition. However, it is perhaps much more fruitful to see the relation as dynamic, a productive tension between two extremes of the same logic, albeit differentiated culturally and historically depending on which particular epic is being discussed. This is an important caveat, because for most of us in the twenty-first century epic in the traditional sense has become an unfamiliar form. In popular usage, in a return to the communal roots of the term, 'epic' is an adjective that is applied to any grand sweeping narrative in a multitude of possible forms: film; television; the novel; role-playing and computer games, all have their own epic productions. Range, scope and sheer size define what can be described as epic. This element of ancient and classical epic has served to become its most significant defining feature.

This volume seeks to trace the history of this shift while at the same time making the various texts and forms accessible. The process of change is very uneven, much more so than the schematic history initially laid out here. But it should be possible to chart the various ways in which the standing of epic forms is affected. There are two major considerations. The first is the relationship between a given epic form or work and the culture within and for which it was produced. The second is the subsequent history of that same work when it is appropriated, reinvented, subsumed, consumed or even ultimately marginalised and forgotten by later cultures.

ANCIENT AND CLASSICAL EPIC

The earliest literary culture for which we have any evidence at all, and not only in relation to the epic, is that of the Sumerians. Their rise to prominence during the fourth millennium BCE in what is now southern Iraq led to the emergence of a literate class of nobles and priests, along with a subset of travelling merchants. However, very little remains of their writing except in fragmentary form, although what does exist gives a sense of an emerging set of literary traditions. These are available not just in authoritative forms. Stories, including the epic, act as templates to be varied according to local reinterpretations. Right from the beginning of the history of the epic, then, there is interplay across culturally defined notions of authority as these narratives migrate and are reinvented. A.E. George discusses the variant versions of *Gilgamesh* written in the later Old Babylonian language as follows:

> Altogether these eleven Old Babylonian manuscripts provide several disconnected episodes in a little over six hundred lines of poetry.

> Some of these lines are from passages that describe the same episode slightly differently, so it transpires that the eleven manuscripts are not witnesses to a single edition of the poem, but to at least two and probably more. There is not enough shared text to determine how extensive the differences are, but it is already clear that we can speak both of distinct recensions (where the differences are minor) and of distinct versions (where the differences are major).
>
> (George 2010: 4)

George's analysis accounts for multiple textual variants across the region, so much so that it makes little sense to assume an originary, unitary source. There is plenty of room for manoeuvre as elements of oral narrative intertwine with written forms; George reminds us that the literary forms are not themselves entirely fixed. In the introduction to her collection of Mesopotamian texts for the Oxford World's Classics (Dalley 2008: xv–xix), Stephanie Dalley provides an accessible overview in which she emphasises that the written forms we have are the result of a two part inter-related process. She discerns the emergence of a conception of textual authority, albeit one that is still relatively fluid. She also notes that there are culturally and socially sanctioned scribal variations. This produces a situation in which later writers are expected to play with the traditional stories, although still broadly within the parameters of a mostly oral culture.

We know about the Sumerian antecedents mostly from their influence upon their successors, the Akkadians. They came from the more northerly parts of Mesopotamia and took over the territory of their southern cousins. We are on much firmer ground here and enough survives in tablets using cuneiform writing for scholars to reconstruct entire stories, including epics. Fragments from various sites enable us to build up a picture of how literary fluidity comes into existence. The evidence demonstrates that traditional stories in both oral and written forms were expected to be reworked and reworded. As an oral form in the first instance, later written versions of epic will be historically specific, marked by contingency in the form of local variations on a theme, in much the same way that diverse versions of a myth can be found in different places. Also, and equally important, has been the discovery of multiple copies of exactly the same texts in several locations, enabling reasonably accurate transcriptions to be produced by piecing together a particular narrative. What is missing from one version can be supplemented by a fragment from somewhere else.

Dalley describes the overall contextual dynamic between oral and written forms as "inventive competition" (Dalley 2008: xv). It is clear that two overlapping cultural imperatives are at work here: poetic innovation and (at the same time) faithful textual transmission. She provides several instances of the process at work in her notes to the various texts. The overall narrative is reconstituted from these versions into the form that is recognisable in most modern editions. For example, the emergence of the wild man Enkidu to challenge the great hero-king Gilgamesh is followed by their friendship and quest. After Enkidu's death Gilgamesh goes on his solitary journey to discover the secret of immortality, in the course of which he meets the legendary survivor of the great flood. Eventually he returns home without immortality, but content to live out his life as the founder of the Sumerian city of Uruk. Diverse texts are put together to produce the standardised version of *Gilgamesh* and Dalley is careful to note the divergences:

> [...] at this point the relationship between Gilgamesh and Enkidu is that of master and servant, as in the Sumerian stories of Gilgamesh, whereas in the rest of the Akkadian epic they are equal comrades. However, later in this tablet Gilgamesh is called Enkidu's brother.
>
> (Dalley 2008: 134, n.150)

In an early section, therefore, Gilgamesh is Enkidu's social superior. Later on, however, the same 'text' represents them as equals. The precise nature of the bond between Gilgamesh and the epic's other main hero Enkidu is open to multiple interpretations. Such textual variation even on the same tablet may well seem alien to a later culture, but it should be remembered that it takes a great degree of sophistication for such a wide range of possibilities to be produced.

Similar comments could be made in relation to the construction of the Sanskrit epics of the *Ramayana* and the *Mahabharata*. Joshua T. Katz compares these poems with the Western epic tradition in much the same way that Jack Goody evaluates the epic productions of Homeric Greek culture by means of comparison with African oral storytelling traditions (Katz 2009: 20–30). Such a comparative methodology suggests useful points about the oral traditions that lie behind literary epic texts. In the case of the *Mahabharata* and the *Ramayana*, John Brockington indicates how they comprise much more than literary texts that are underpinned by their oral predecessors in a direct linear and stable inheritance. Both are subjected to a long process of rewriting, and in the case of the *Mahabharata* in particular, massive expansion (Brockington 1998: 130–58). The situation of the *Ramayana* is slightly different, partly because its text reaches a relatively stable form earlier than the *Mahabharata* (Brockington 1998: 377–97).

The Indian epics provide a useful point of comparison with the two major narrative strands of Sumerian and then Akkadian epic. The much earlier Mesopotamian stories comprise a series of themes, some of which are better known than others. For example, although *Gilgamesh* makes reference to the traditional story of a great flood, that event is represented as having taken place at some unspecified point in the past. However, the narrative of *Gilgamesh* is now less well-known than the story of the flood, due to its dissemination through the much later Hebrew Bible and beyond into Christian tradition. The basic *motif* is that of the divinely inspired survival of the one true man and his family, and the result of this cataclysm is effectively a second creation. The earliest version we have, in Old Babylonian, comes from around 1700 BCE and it already demonstrates themes that are well-known from the much later Old Testament *Book of Genesis*. It incorporates a creation myth, human overpopulation, a God's decision to wipe out humanity, the saving of one wise man (Atrahasis) and his family, and a second creation of humanity via the descendants of Atrahasis. Two main differences from the more familiar Biblical story of Noah need to be noted. The first is that in the *Atrahasis* the catastrophe does not come about as a direct result of the concept of original sin. The second is that as a reward for his piety and wisdom, Atrahasis is blessed with outright immortality. He represents the pinnacle of human achievement and is rewarded accordingly. Stephanie Dalley notes that an alternative view might be that when humanity was initially created, it was not only able to breed prodigiously, but was also immortal (Dalley 2008: 2–8). The resulting overpopulation led to a divine decision to send the flood as a means of correcting an error in creation, but that the sole survivor of antediluvian humanity, Atrahasis, remains naturally immortal. In this reading, the second creation of humanity rectifies the original error by making all subsequent humans mortal. During his wanderings, the hero Gilgamesh meets with the same personage, although in that poem he goes by the name Utnapishtim. This allows some of the flood story to be incorporated into *Gilgamesh* as the recounting of prior events by one of the participants (Dalley 2008: 4–6).

Between them, these two stories supply us with early evidence of major epic *motifs*, as well as literary techniques such as the internal story or sub-narrative. In this way, elements that are perhaps more familiar from the Greek and Roman classics can be discerned in their predecessors. The salient features include struggle and battle, the achievement of great deeds, the perilous journey, the appearance of supernatural and divine elements, the semi-divine importance of the great hero, and the importance of emulation between heroes that leads both to friendship and conflict. Stylistic aspects include tropes such as epithets, extended similes and the threefold repetition of dreams. In John Miles Foley's *A Companion to Ancient Epic*, Richard P. Martin fully discusses such defining generic traits in ancient epic in his essay "Epic as Genre" (Martin 2009), as does Jack M. Sasson in his essay "Comparative Observations on the Near Eastern Epic Traditions" in the same volume (Sasson 2009). Both accounts include the identification of poetic form and the establishment of typological categories in their definitions of epic and their analyses of how epic works for a given culture. In their different ways both insist upon the integral nature of the relationship between an epic and its culture, as opposed to a universal formal and generic definition that is trans-cultural. The epic fulfils a social function, and one of the variations that will inevitably occur is that between the oral and the literary, which is fruitfully investigated by Jack Goody. This may be the most efficient way to think of epic, because it allows for such variations as well as examples of specific kinds of practice. It also offers a means of untangling the dense intermingling of communal and literary forms that comprises epic production. Attention inevitably focuses upon the uses of epic in ways that allow each manifestation to be analysed on a case by case basis, according to their historical, cultural and social specificity. This is a different emphasis from that taken by the famous French anthropologist, Claude Lévi-Strauss. Laurence Coupe sums up his structuralist view of myth as follows: "[…] in his hands each myth turns out to be about the code of every myth, the metalanguage which conforms and constrains all tellings of tales" (Coupe 2009: 140–1). In his books *Structural Anthropology* and *Myth and Meaning*, Lévi-Strauss refines the range of myth-based narratives down to a series of types, which he relates to a basic encounter between culture and nature. Coupe's claim is that the correlations between myth cycles from different cultures can be fruitfully compared, without necessarily referring back to some deep structural universal truth (Coupe 2009: 138–48). This comparative methodology would apply to epic as well as to other forms.

Another major advantage of a historically-based analysis of this kind is that it provides a dynamic awareness of social change. It accounts for the ways in which the more immediate inheritors of the Sumerian and Akkadian tradition simultaneously use and rework epic for their own ends. As time progresses, the local variations that are already familiar from the earlier periods begin to take on associations that could be regarded as part of a longer process of nation-building. As a sense of shared cultural identity begins to emerge, communal activities such as the production of epic can later be appropriated for nationalistic purposes. A community can attempt to redefine itself in relation to the myths and legends of its own past through the medium of the epic, while at the same time enacting its epic as a form exclusive to itself. This is a development of the process of reworking and modification that already existed in earlier Sumerian and Akkadian epic. However, it is one that appropriates the epic for a very specific set of purposes.

It is important to note that even as these ancient manifestations of epic develop, the narrative forms adopted are relatively loose and episodic. A useful example of the process can be discerned in the aggrandisement of Marduk in the Babylonian *Epic of Creation* (c. 1200 BCE) especially in the final stages of the poem. By this point in the narrative Marduk is triumphant and the epic becomes almost a ritual recounting, a litany of his titles (Dalley 2008: 231–2). This kind of listing of elements is common enough in previous epics, such as the descriptions of the attainments of Gilgamesh, but here the narrative logic is extended. This particular epic is not only about struggle and conflict, but the celebration of the powerful position that emerges from it. Much of the poem is given over to this element in a way that was not the case in earlier epics. By way of comparison, it is possible to read the *Tora* (*Pentateuch*) as performing the same function for the Hebrews. There the overall narrative of the wanderings and tribulations of the Jews leads to the final conquest of the promised land (Niditch 2009), but this narrative is punctuated with extensive recounting of the patriarchal lineages, exhaustive descriptions of the construction of the ark of the covenant, and the elaboration of the laws of God.

A different form of heroic characterisation emerges in Homeric epic, which had a similar importance for the Greeks who succeeded the Mycenaeans of the Trojan War. The Homeric works (*The Iliad* and *The Odyssey*) do not lead up to the founding of a community in the Mosaic mould, but are of crucial importance to Greek identity as cultured inheritors of a great tradition. In terms of later reception and transmission of the Homeric texts, Aristotle is of particular importance, although it should be noted that by his time (384–322 BCE) the tradition has become a literary one based on a different set of criteria from earlier, looser narratives (Martin 2009: 11). In *The Poetics* (c. 335 BCE) Aristotle is very careful to differentiate epic from tragedy by privileging the latter: "[...] all the elements of epic are found in tragedy, though not everything that belongs to tragedy is to be found in epic" (Aristotle 1985: 38). Accordingly, since tragedy is all-inclusive whereas epic is not, the theatrical form is to be preferred to the poetic. Tragedy is also superior to the epic in the way that it keeps to the unities of time, plot and place and, crucially, because it has an even tighter narrative format than epic (Aristotle 1985: 68). The Greek theorist rounds off his comparison of the two forms by stating that "there is less unity in the imitation of the epic poets" (Aristotle 1985: 75). Aristotle's privileging of unity inevitably relegates epic to second place behind tragedy because epic imitation of action is more episodic than in tragedy.

The Hellenistic poet Apollonius of Rhodes (early third century BCE) self-consciously develops the associations generated by Aristotle's inflection of Homeric epic in his *Argonautica* (c. 260 BCE). Apollonius builds directly upon Aristotle's privileging of narrative unity by elaborating upon the poetic narrative persona, the first person singular of direct authorial statement. Subsequently, the Roman poet Virgil expands this rhetorical device in the *Aeneid* (written from 29–19 BCE), although for different reasons. Virgil inflects his work with a very precise literary posture, a developmental form of authorial identity that he finds in his immediate predecessor, Lucretius (c. 100–50 BCE). In Virgil's formulation, the poet represents himself as self-consciously elaborating his craft, experimenting with various devices until he attains the apogee of the epic form. He does this right at the beginning of the *Aeneid,* producing a resolutely literary posture that fully extends the literary element present in the earliest epic forms, at the expense of the more inclusive, communal oral elements. Virgil refers to his career prior to his taking on the subject matter of the founding of Rome, and his statement comes before the invocation to the muse with which the poem proper begins.

At the same time, however, Virgil clothes the literary epic tradition he inherits from the Greeks in the garb of Roman imperialism. Since the poem is produced at the moment of the political shift from republic to empire, the *Aeneid* reworks the founding myth of the Roman people. Jasper Griffin's introduction to C. Day Lewis' translation of the poem shows how

Virgil's poem appropriates the Homeric tradition for Roman culture, directing it towards Augustus as head of the House of the Julii, descended from Aeneas (Griffin 2008: ix–xiv). David Quint analyses in detail this complex process of cultural appropriation: "The epic victors both project their present power prophetically into the future and trace its legitimating origins back into the past" (Quint 1993: 45). For Quint, this is a very powerful defining moment in the history of the development of European epic. Virgilian epic offers a narrative history that is ideologically inflected in that it is steeped in the politics of Augustan Rome. However, Quint also notes that other possibilities remain open even within Virgil's conflation of epic form and imperial power:

> Epic's losers, the enemies of empire whom epic ideology assimilates with the East, woman, nature, irrationality and chaos, consequently also embody a potential, indeed inevitable, collapse of narrative. This is what epic depicts in the undecided suspense and confusion of battle – the endless war that Milton's Satan would prolong into eternity – and in the circuitous wanderings of romance.
>
> (Quint 1993: 45)

For Quint, therefore, Virgil inaugurates a narrative of *imperium* that will resonate powerfully through the entire literary tradition that comes after him.

Quint begins his account by analysing the crucial narrative and historical importance of Aeneas' shield. He sees the depiction of the flight of Cleopatra and Antony from the Battle of Actium as the culminating moment of the Roman Civil Wars and this representation serves to inaugurate the tropes of subversive femininity and the oriental 'other' that Shakespeare later drew upon in *Antony and Cleopatra* (c. 1608). The image on Aeneas' shield conforms to the requirements of Augustan propaganda by working to efface the fact that Actium was part of a civil war. This representation of power requires the production of victims. The losers in the struggle, Cleopatra and Antony, are misrepresented as marginalised 'others' in the face of the symbolic centrality of Augustan Rome.

Virgil therefore produces a powerful narrative of empire, subsuming epic into the political demands of an imperial project. However, what this tradition inaugurates contains other possibilities that later epics explore. Quint detects a reaction against this Virgilian appropriation of the epic in Lucan's *Pharsalia* (c. 61 CE), which looks back to the struggle that culminated in the ascendancy of Julius Caesar. Lucan's position is sympathetic to the last generation of Republicans, even as he acknowledges their weaknesses in the face of Caesarean imperialism. Shadi Bartsch traces this sympathy to Lucan's own direct involvement in Roman politics under Nero, which cost him his life (Bartsch 2009). For Quint, Lucan's engagement with both politics and the literary form of the epic produces a duality within the Western tradition; henceforth, any given epic poem will be defined over and against its treatment of empire. It is possible to find elements of epic counter-narrative in writers such as Statius (c. 45–96 CE), who follows Lucan's lead in engaging directly with the Virgilian identification of epic with empire. These debates over cultural identity will feed into the redevelopment of romance and epic forms during the European Middle Ages, with the caveat that romance emerges as a subset of Virgilian epic that occasionally contests the dominant epic narrative strategy. The migration of narratives has its own history, and it is inevitably one of ideologically inflected representation. So much so indeed that with European epic after Virgil, every individual epic is always politically and historically overdetermined in very specific ways.

FROM THE HEROIC TOWARDS ROMANCE AND ALLEGORY

It is possible to see the *Aeneid* as a rewriting of the relationship between the hero and the community. David Quint goes so far as to suggest that Virgil's poem performs a reverse operation on the self-sufficient identity of the Homeric heroes (Quint 1993: 84–92), with the result that independent action becomes almost impossible for Aeneas. Thus, when Virgil identifies epic directly with the imperial interest, he does so by subordinating the figure of the hero to the needs of the state. His successors inflect their own versions of this relationship in different ways, often varying according to the extent of their reliance on the Virgilian model.

However, this is not the only paradigm that existed for the various epic forms that proliferated in the centuries following the demise of the Western Roman Empire. For many of these cultures, heroic epic functions at the intersection of the relationship between the individual and the community. Richard M. Dorson characterises the ways in which such a confluence opens up the epic as a form of shared experience, which of course reinforces its roots in communal myth-making (Dorson 1977). It could be said that this strand of epic production stands at the opposite extreme from those writers who continue to follow the post-Virgilian classical tradition.

There are many variations among the most well-known 'heroic' epics of the period known in Europe as the Middle Ages. *Beowulf*, which was written sometime between the eighth and early eleventh centuries, is a case in point. Unlike *The Iliad*, the poem's title directly refers to the eponymous hero at the centre of the narrative. This poem and others such as the Middle English *Sir Orfeo* (c.1400 CE), could be seen to develop a strand of epic story-making that can be traced through *The Odyssey* to *Gilgamesh*. Roberta Frank shows how the *Beowulf* poet is not conscious of a great epic tradition except in so far as his own culture imagines its own legendary past (Frank 2002). By way of comparison, the romance tradition reworks a semi-mythical past by means of identifiable literary *motifs* such as the knightly quest and the intricacies of courtly love. This can be seen in the ways that *Sir Orfeo* rewrites the Orpheus myth in order to manage concerns that are historically and culturally specific to the time of the later poem. For example, *Sir Orfeo* incorporates the old epic element of the journey to the underworld in displaced form, but it is flavoured with the familiar quests so beloved of the troubadour romances.

The growing importance of the Christian religion during the first millennium results in its own epic narratives, perhaps the most well-known of which is Dante's *Divine Comedy* (written between 1308 and 1321). But it would be misleading to characterise this development as a smooth process. The medieval inscription of epic refurbishes prior non-Christian and earlier Christian tales with a veneer derived from a later Christian *ethos*, especially by means of allegory. The Italian Christian humanist rediscovery of the classics is epitomised in Dante's project. However, this process of textual transmission is not uniform or unproblematic, and crucial variations appear in particular instances. For example, the medieval manuscripts that preserve early Irish epics struggle to produce a composite picture of a resolutely Celtic pre-Christian world. So too the collection of tales that will later be gathered together in the *Mabinogion* (c. 1325) can be re-read as a memorialisation of the encounter between Celtic and Druidic myth and Christianity, without necessarily privileging the one over the other. It is possible to see the Norse-Icelandic sagas as evincing similar concerns, and all of these cultures owe very little to the legacy of the classical model.

These particularly well-known examples notwithstanding, it should also be remembered that the genre is not confined to Europe. While it would be difficult to characterise the *Arabian Nights* as an epic, it nevertheless has a place in its own culture that is equivalent to the function of epic in Western culture. A better known avowedly epic poem from outside Europe is the retrospective Iranian *Shah-Namah* (c. 1000 CE). This narrative reworks the histories of the dynasties of kings through the lens of later Persian contemporary concerns. An epic oral tradition is also to be found in Mongolia and has such cultural prestige that Chao Gejin characterises it as "[...] the most important genre in Mongolian literary history" (Gejin 1997: 322). Such comparisons indicate that epic cannot be reduced to a singular form.

In many ways, however, these various epic narratives share certain concerns as well as incorporating elements that are unique to their own particular cultures. One of the most important is the way in which a given epic will manage its engagement with the heroic past. Epic of this kind is not simply a retelling of legendary events; it opens up those occurrences and their heroes to critique. Thus, in the Old French *Chansons de Geste*, the manuscript versions of which date from the middle of the twelfth century onwards, the audience is invited to imagine its own relationship to the events and personages being represented from the past. In the case of the Icelandic sagas, a similar operation takes on the function of a myth of origins. The great deeds and struggles of the hero make perfect sense but so too do the mistakes that are made, or the inability of the hero (or heroes) to gain their stated aim. Romance takes this logic even further by making the obstacles and encounters that litter the hero's path central to the narrative.

THE RENAISSANCE AND THE EARLY NOVEL

The logic of the romance diverges from that of epic more generally, creating a multiplicity of treatments of epic *motifs* as the medieval *ethos* gradually shades into the Renaissance. Additionally, the prose novel begins to be fashioned from more rough and ready popular narrative materials as well as from the *detritus* of epic. The combination demonstrates the continuing power and usefulness of the epic, as its rhetorical forms migrate towards the new hybrid narratives. This suggests a rather conflicted field of enquiry, so it is perhaps more useful to think of multiple developments in the influence of epic, rather than of some kind of overarching explanatory grand narrative. Any such narrative will have to account for the ways in which the Renaissance occurs at different times in different places, as waves of Italian influence make their way northwards to countries such as England. Boiardo, Ariosto and Tasso are particularly important in this respect, as they use allegory to fuse medieval romance with humanism in their Orlando stories. In an essay entitled "Italian Renaissance Epic", Giuseppe Mazotta characterises these Italian Renaissance writers as producing a "hybrid form" (Mazotta 2010: 95):

> Their poems cannot be termed simply 'epics'. We designate them epic romances: a sort of mixed or hybrid genre that develops from the countless vulgarizations and adaptations of the *Chanson de Roland* in Franco-Italian and Franco-Venetian circles.
>
> (Mazotta 2010: 96)

The Italian poets manage to do so by commingling the epic tradition derived from Old French poems with the Arthurian romance tradition. This new wave of epic-style production in turn exerts great influence on later European writers.

Spenser is a case in point. The *Faerie Queene* (1590–6) is marked by fidelity to the principles of the reformation. Spenser follows the Italians in his use of allegory, but situates it within a newly Protestant context. Catherine Bates relates the experience of writing and reading Spenser's work to an emerging set of disciplined reading practices, conditioned by direct engagement with the Bible as a text (Bates 2010: 137). She also notes how the poem's nationalist elements begin to emerge; her essay is entitled "*The Faerie Queene*: Britain's National Monument". Here, she argues that Spenser negotiates a space for his national epic between the realities of Elizabethan courtly life and legendary figures such as King Arthur and Redcrosse Knight, or St George, England's patron saint. Nascent Protestant imperialism is the emerging context for Spenser's work, and he recuperates the Virgilian classical models of poetic development from eclogue and pastoral allegory to epic narratives of nationalist heroism.

The same posture is resolutely taken up by the later, even more radical figure of Milton. David Quint argues that Milton marks a limit point for the poetic epic in English (Quint 1993) in that he tries to produce his Christian epic by integrating his narrative with a form that has so many pagan and classical associations, a Protestant version of the synthesis achieved by Dante, and developed with a different emphasis by Spenser. For Quint, and as romantic poets such as Coleridge discovered later, Milton's achievement was such that it made epic poetry almost impossible thereafter. Other critics have also made this point, perhaps the most well-known of which is Harold Bloom in *The Anxiety of Influence* (Bloom 1997: 20–5). He describes *Paradise Lost* as:

> [...] an allegory of the dilemma of the modern poet, at his strongest. Satan is that modern poet, while God is his dead but still embarrassingly potent and present ancestor, or rather, ancestral poet. Adam is the potentially strong modern poet, but at his weakest moment, when he has yet to find his own voice.

> (Bloom 1997: 20)

Bloom conceives poetic creation as an Oedipal struggle to locate the point at which poets resist and then overcome their patriarchal predecessors, and he regards *Paradise Lost* as a kind of limit text in its unusual manifestation of ancestral patriarchal authority that later poetic offspring had difficulty in overcoming. He uses an aggressively masculine vocabulary that emphasises strength and weakness as defining poetic characteristics. His masculinist question "For why do men write poems?" (Bloom 1997: 22), clearly excludes female writers and when he reaches the nineteenth century, he defines writers such as Coleridge and Hopkins as: "Poets this late in tradition are both Adams and Satans. They begin as natural men [...]" (Bloom 1997: 24). Bloom's sense of the patriarchal power embodied in Milton's writing inevitably renders the poetry of those who come later relatively weak by comparison.

It is still possible, however, to locate Milton in relation to literary developments in his own time. As well as massive compositions that defy easy classification, such as Rabelais' *Gargantua and Pantagruel* (1532 onwards) in France, there is also Sidney's classical aristocratic prose Romance, the *Arcadia* (started in the late 1570s). With the publication of *Don Quixote* in Spain (vol. 1 1605, vol. 2 1615), the developing history of the early novel produces a movement that is as uneven and conflicted as the issues encountered by the epic in the sixteenth century. The productive tension that is engendered by the arrival of the novel includes its interrogation of epic forms and *motifs* such as the parody of the quest in *Don Quixote*. This inaugural moment feeds into the picaresque novel's fascination with characters and situations from lower points on the social scale than are usually found in epic. Such works as Defoe's *Moll Flanders* (1722) or Sterne's later *Sentimental Journey* (1768) manage their plotlines and characterisations by deploying devices that are already familiar from the epic, such as the journey or voyage, as well as techniques of episodic narration. The result is that a new literary energy erupts from the mannered world of the humanist epic and drives the genre forward. The major historical event that made this revolution possible was the invention of the printing press, which democratised reading and exposed readers to new literary forms.

As a result, the novel opens literary writing up to an expanding readership. In her book, *Mothers of the Novel*, Dale Spender explores how women in particular were able to take advantage of this phenomenon (Spender 1986). Aphra Behn's *Oroonoko* (1688) is one of the most famous early manifestations of this historic shift, especially in the ways it integrates women's writing with the emergence of narratives of colonisation.

EPIC IN THE AGE OF THE INDIVIDUAL

Poetry continues to be the preserve of a well-educated elite for several centuries after the Renaissance. Despite this the classics continue to exert an influence mainly through institutions such as schools and universities. A useful example can be found in the work of Alexander Pope. His mock heroics *The Rape of the Lock* (1712) and *The Dunciad* (first published in 1728) are directed primarily to a readership steeped in the classical forms, since in order for his satire to work, the reader needs to understand the primary features of epic. This is not only a case of assumed familiarity with the kinds of topics that appear in epic. The works are structured fully in accordance with *motifs* familiar from Virgil such as the invocation to the muse and narratives of conflict and battle. Pope's ability to entertain his highly literate readership by using such techniques demonstrates the existence of a widespread awareness of the conventions of epic.

Overall, however, there is a relative decline in the quantity and quality of epic poetry when compared with its cultural importance in the Renaissance. Even so, it would be an error to assume that the practice of a socially involved form like the epic became entirely impossible. It is during the Augustan and Romantic periods that the national epic develops logically from the Virgilian identification of the form with the state, although it has to be remembered that the British Romantics produced a number of incomplete or failed epics. Coleridge, Wordsworth and Byron all seem to have been unable to inhabit the epic with any success, perhaps because of their emphasis on the importance of the individual creative imagination. This suggestion recalls David Quint's observation that the *Aeneid* subsumes the hero's identity within the larger destiny of the state, something that the Romantics could not easily reconcile with their focus on individualism.

Writers who remain more within the mainstream of epic production along the lines of the Virgilian model would include MacPherson and his publication of the supposed works of Ossian in 1765. His timing was excellent, in that it permitted him to capitalise upon the contemporary question of Scotland's status in the union, especially after the failed rising of 1745. The "rediscovered" works of an early Scottish bard found a ready audience. The debate that followed concerning the authenticity of the works of Ossian can be understood in terms of an already existing receptive and appropriately primed readership. This is particularly important for the relationship between epic narrative and ideas of national identity. A point of comparison would be the exiled Polish poet Mickiewicz (1798–1855), who has come to characterise the Polish response to Romantic imperatives. The partitioning of Poland between Prussia, Austria-Hungary and Russia provided an impetus for the growth of Romantic Polish nationalism. Perhaps more well known, in Britain at least, is the Finnish *Kalevala*, which was constructed almost entirely consciously as a refashioning of folk tales into something approaching a national epic. When Yeats later adopted a similar procedure in Ireland, he was simply adapting the same logic to his own situation. Each of these poets demonstrates the continued vitality of the link between the epic form and nationalist imperatives.

The narrative antecedents of the developing form of the novel exposed it to epic influences, even though the solitary action of reading a novel seems to be the antithesis of the latent communal element of epic production. For example, the epic *motif* of the journey migrates into the *picaresque* novel, providing works such as Fielding's *Tom Jones* (1749) with material for a whole series of comic inversions. A prime example comes in Chapter 8 of Book 4 of *Tom Jones*, when Molly Seagrim's fight is rendered in mock heroic style (Fielding 1985: 141–3). Richardson's *Pamela* (1740) reworks traditional gender stereotypes, which in turn generates debates internal to the novel form. Fielding's *Shamela* (1741) deliberately satirises Richardson's representation of women.

With the continued development of the novel's popularity, a very wide range of publishing techniques emerged, particularly in the nineteenth century. The serialisation of novels in journals and newspapers demonstrates this form's widely enhanced social role and importance, underpinning the great success enjoyed by Dickens at public readings in Britain and America. If epic is again considered to be a function rather than a form, the grand sweeping narratives so beloved of nineteenth-century novelists can be described as epics in their own right. Epic, it would appear, can take various forms. Well-established elements of epic that are familiar from the outset, such as the presence of, or allusion to, the supernatural, the heroic struggle, the epithet or physical description, become extremely important for novelists. In this respect it is possible to see the huge novels of the eighteenth and nineteenth centuries as embodying concerns that are already familiar in poetic epic, even as they do so in ways that are pertinent to their own cultural and historical environment.

The novel turns out to be capable of taking on epic themes and proportions of its own. Tolstoy used it to characterise the grand sweep of Napoleonic history in *War and Peace* (first published in 1869) and to investigate the relationship between the individual and society in *Anna Karenina* (1873–7). His contemporary Fyodor Dostoevsky used the conventions of the realist novel to focus upon character psychology in *Crime and Punishment* (1866) and *The Brothers Karamazov* (1880); both of these novels saw initial publication in serial form.

The advent of Modernism leads to a direct and full engagement with the epic. This may be a result of the importance of symbolism for the Modernists, as an intensification of the techniques of allegory that had characterised medieval and Renaissance epic and romance. Perhaps the most well-known modern epic is Joyce's *Ulysses* (first published in serial form, from 1918–20), but he is not the only writer to return to the structure of the Homeric original. In Greece, Nikos Kazantzakis does something similar through the medium of poetry. Unlike Joyce, who structures his novel in direct correspondence with the *Odyssey*, Kazantzakis writes his work as a sequel. Both of these writers owe a great debt to epic form, although they adopt different ways of relating to it.

Where Joyce integrates the structure of the Homeric poem into his novel, Kazantzakis departs from it entirely in his production of a new narrative. The Modernist moment of the reinterpretation of the epic past therefore works as a form of engagement, a renegotiation that results in much more than simply a repetition of epic devices and narrative forms.

Post-colonial challenges to imperial power became an important focus for the Caribbean poet Derek Walcott. For him, the reinterpretation of Homer's works constitutes a crucial moment of contact between the West and its others. In his *Omeros* (1990), Walcott extends the range of reference to aspects of culture previously excluded from literary representation. Walcott engages with the end of empire, class politics and gendered representation. These concerns also appear in the Canadian writer Margaret Atwood's feminist engagement with the *Odyssey* in *The Penelopiad* (2005). By rewriting the story of Odysseus in order to place Penelope at the centre of her novel, Atwood makes clear the enduring influence of such generically and gender-marked master narratives, as well as the need to react against them, rework them and reinterpret them.

At the same time as these texts appear, the waning of the twentieth century sees the appropriation of epic by a host of new genres and media. Film and television return to 'epic' stories taken from the Bible, Homer and classical drama. The explosion of fantasy and science fiction writing also feeds into the new media. As a relatively accessible narrative form, epic is colonised, appropriated and reworked by all of these various genres. Some of the terms are suggestive: the 'space opera' of the Golden Age of Science Fiction (E.E. 'Doc' Smith); the emergence of 'heroic fantasy' (Robert E. Howard; Fritz Leiber and others); and overtly epic novels and series (Tolkien; Frank Herbert and Michael Moorcock). The veritable explosion of writing that explicitly concerns itself with alternative realities takes the epic form in new directions, although of course some of the writers involved do share the political interests of Walcott, or of Atwood.

The performance arts also re-appropriate the epic, as evidenced in the theory and dramaturgy of Bertolt Brecht. He shows that the epic is available to media other than poetry or the novel, with which it was identified for so long. In a sense, he also returns the epic to its communal roots in performance culture. The explicit political emphasis that is a crucial element of Brecht's epic theatre is perhaps even more important, and by removing epic from its association with the imperial state, he opens it up to a radical engagement with alternative political formations. Brecht's involvement with German Expressionism, and his use of filmic techniques such as montage, aligns epic with the visual vocabulary of the new forms of cinema and then television. Mankiewicz's film of Shakespeare's *Julius Caesar* (1953) exemplifies some of the ways in which Expressionist techniques infiltrate mainstream Hollywood, an engagement with Shakespeare as high culture that parallels the grand biblical and 'swords and sandals' epics associated with North American Hollywood directors such as Cecil B. DeMille. Television series such as *Star Trek* and film series such as *Star Wars* embody a range of recognisable epic *motifs*: the voyage of exploration, the struggle against greater, almost supernatural powers, and the journey towards self-discovery by the central hero. More recently and in the wake of *Star Trek*, *Babylon 5* reworks science fiction on television as a post-colonial narrative, with its central story arc of the struggle of younger races like humanity against its elders, who are themselves embroiled in an ancient cosmic conflict. The term most often associated with such works is 'saga', a direct appropriation of Icelandic epics via televised novels such as Galsworthy's *Forsyte Saga*. In these examples, epic form is therefore appropriated by radically different media, and presumably its use in this popular context is intended to lend epic *gravitas* to its subject matter.

The availability of new media recalls the emergence and consolidation of the novel, in that new epic structures can and do come into being in later periods as a consequence of new technologies. An excellent example is the slow emergence of children's epic as it has evolved from children's tales to the complex multi-volume narratives of writers such as Philip Pullman. Pullman's *His Dark Materials* trilogy (1995–2000) reworks the terrain of C.S. Lewis' seven *Narnia* books (1949–54) by explicitly removing the pseudo-Christian *ethos* that is so important for the earlier writer. The epic *motif* of the journey to discovery of new truths is central to Pullman's work, although his narratives are recast to dispense with divinity.

It remains yet to be seen how many of these newer groupings manage to deploy epic forms and *motifs* and extend their usefulness. Even so, there are already tantalising glimpses of new modes of accessibility, since in the wake of the rapid development of computer technology, desk-top publishing makes it possible for almost anyone to become a writer. This not only applies to literary forms; it has also seen the emergence of new kinds of entertainment that actively engage with the creative possibilities associated with aspects of the epic. These new media draw on existing cultural forms, resulting in computer games versions of the 'sagas' and in series derived from other media, such as the *Star Wars* franchise. One computer games company, LucasArts, was originally a spin-off from the motion picture special effects unit of Industrial Light & Magic. In these programs, players are given the opportunity to become personally involved in developing storylines that are built into the premise of each individual game. Epic narratives exist in various forms within the various genres of computer games; for example, in the *Wing Commander* series of space pilot games, the individual missions are subsumed into an evolving heroic struggle that has grown as the series matures. In these games, the narrative is predicated upon an all-out war between humanity and a feline race called the Kilrathi, and the actions of the players determine the course of the war. The game reinvents the pivotal importance of the Homeric hero, which has more recently extended into online communities for titles such as *World of Warcraft*.

Non-digital analogue forms are also available, that take their cue from epic elements such as the heroic struggle against powerful enemies, and open them up to both personal and group interaction. The impact of writers such as Tolkien and Moorcock is what lies behind the massive success of the role-playing game genre from the late 1970s, with its beginnings in *Chainmail* and *Dungeons & Dragons*. The line of descent is very clear: epic forms such as the Norse sagas influenced modern literary writers, who in turn inspire the writers of these games. Other sophisticated forms quickly emerged in many different genres, ranging from space opera through modern horror and various kinds of historical setting. It is possible for a group of friends and a decent umpire to engage in a form of collective myth-making via an epic role-playing campaign series. It is now even possible for players to act out their roles in person, with the growth of live role-playing in its various formats, engaging sub-cultures such as the gothic and the historical re-enactor. In these versions, people dress as their characters and enact scenarios designed either as stand-alone adventures or as part of an ongoing 'campaign'. This is not epic storytelling in a communal setting, but it is recognisably a direct lineal descendant of the form, and it enables the participants to construct their own epic. This feature permits a form of post-modern performativity to appropriate the epic in especially distinct ways.

The sheer variety of different forms and possibilities is impressive, but what matter here are the ways in which these various sub-genres utilise the energies and *motifs* that already exist in epic forms. They appropriate and discard the various components they need in a way that problematises any easy division between the purely personal and the socially complex. Modern audiences interact with aspects of epic but they do so in ways that would perhaps seem alien to their forebears. Epic may no longer always be easily available to modern consumers in its traditional forms, but its components continue to resonate, even if they do so in relatively fragmented ways.

2

ANCIENT AND CLASSICAL EPIC

The earliest fragmentary remains of written epic constitute a subset of writing in general. However, enough cuneiform versions of various stories remain to enable a provisional reconstruction of an epic tradition to be made. The stories are first encountered in Sumerian versions, which then pass into wider currency later on, especially with the rise of the Akkadians. The prestige of the older language remains, particularly because of its association with the first major cities in Mesopotamia. The cities produce literacy and bureaucracy in equal measure, and the emergence of a scribal priestly class of scholars and officials helps to cement a literary culture.

There are always variations as well as similarities. Multiple versions emerge due to local concerns that may result in the emphasis of different parts of the same general literary tradition. In addition, local frames of reference are expected of the performer who narrates an epic tale. The earliest epic forms are nonetheless inscribed within a very specific relationship between the verbal and the written, between the culture that produces an epic tale and that which writes it down; the two need not necessarily be coterminous. But at the same time the peculiarities of this relationship need not be ascribed to a simple opposition between speech and writing; indeed what emerges is a dynamic relationship between the two that can be oppositional at times, but can also be complementary.

SUMERIAN AND AKKADIAN EPIC

An accessible description of the rather complicated textual history of the epic of *Atrahasis* is given by Stephanie Dalley. The Old Babylonian version is inscribed on both sides of three clay tablets. There are also several much later Assyrian versions, which include material that does not exist in the older text (Dalley 2008: 3). From the very outset, then, variation is a characteristic feature of the epic. This is inevitable, given the diversity of flood narratives in the region, as Dalley points out:

> It is probable that these ancient Near Eastern flood stories are versions of a tale which originated in lower Mesopotamia, though not necessarily in a single devastation. The variety of detail found in them illustrates the kaleidoscopic character of the folk tale, in which certain basic elements are widely used in new combinations and are adapted to national interests and different literary settings.
>
> (Dalley 2008: 6)

A core tale is easily adaptable, layered with contingent versions of events, flavoured with elements of direct interest to the specific cultural group for which a particular version is produced. The protagonist of the tale does not even have a proper name: 'Atrahasis' is an epithet, meaning the wise one.

The narrative found in the Old Babylonian tablets is straightforward enough. From the beginning, all work is carried out by the gods themselves. When they decide that this is too much for them, they make the Igigi do all the work. It is not clear if these servitor gods already exist or are created specifically for the task; presumably the audience already knows who they are, and so their status is simply taken for granted. During 3,600 years of toil they irrigate the land, dig out the river beds of the Euphrates and the Tigris, and use the soil to build the mountains. Then the

Igigi start to grumble about the workload, as did the gods before them. They confront the major gods and after a great debate designed to avert violence they ask the mother goddess to produce man and the first seven human couples are created. But after 600 years there are too many people and the noise makes the gods regret having created them, so they inflict a series of catastrophes upon humanity. The wise man Atrahasis, who is very close to his god Enki, asks him why the gods are making the people suffer. Each time, Enki tells Atrahasis to manipulate the divine powers by withholding worship from the gods in general, and at the same time making an offering to one in particular. Eventually the gods fall into dissent amongst themselves, and Atrahasis has a dream, which his god Enki interprets for him, commanding him to dismantle his house and build a huge boat from its timbers to save living things. Some of the gods inflict the final doom upon humanity in the form of the great flood, but Atrahasis survives and makes a burnt offering. The savour of his offering reaches the gods, and more dissent is created when Enki says he saved Atrahasis. Eventually a compromise is reached, and Atrahasis lives on.

This necessarily schematic outline anticipates the later version of the story of Noah. Atrahasis is close to his god, he is very clever and he is the recipient of divine dreams. Multiple elements of creation are also incorporated. Unlike the biblical monotheistic version, here the conclave of the gods is divided, but when they eventually come to agreement, post-diluvian history begins. The evolution of this epic narrative strand does not stand in isolation, with elements of it being incorporated into the much longer story of *Gilgamesh*.

The epic of *Gilgamesh* also operates within a partially literary textual tradition, perhaps even more so than the *Atrahasis*. Dalley provides a useful summary of the various versions used by scholars to construct the standard version of the text, noting that the Akkadian versions are thought to have appeared at a date later than the Old Babylonian *Atrahasis*:

> The standard version is the best known, mainly from tablets found at
> Nineveh, which include more than one copy of the work (each with

> different arrangements of tablets and columns). [...] One tablet has more recently come to light from the temple of Nabu at Nimrud. Some school exercise tablets come from the site of Sultantepe near Harrun, dating from the late eighth or seventh century BC.
>
> (Dalley 2008: 46)

Accordingly, the textual history of the two traditions is roughly coterminous, albeit rather complex and stretching over a considerable period.

The figure of Gilgamesh himself is based upon an early tradition of builder-kings, the founders of Sumer's walled cities. In the standard version of the epic story, this personage is responsible for building the walls of Uruk, one of the most important of the first cities. The various texts of *Gilgamesh* combine techniques and *motifs* that are commonly associated with later epics, and which are then usually treated as literary inventions. It is important for the hero to be semi-divine and for him to have a major companion, one who dies before his time. Unlike Patroclus in the *Iliad* or Pallas in the *Aeneid*, however, Enkidu's death by disease is the result of direct divine action. Revenge on a divine perpetrator is not possible, so Gilgamesh displaces his energy and instead sets out on his journey to find the secret of eternal life.

The hero's travels are of course a major element of most epic narratives and *Gilgamesh* is no exception. The difficulty for the literary commentator lies in the supernatural aspect of many epic encounters; at what point is it possible to differentiate between myth and epic, when the epic itself so clearly incorporates mythic material? The creation of Enkidu explicitly connects him with Gilgamesh from the outset; Enkidu is to be the king's wilder counterpart. Of course, in a sense they are both much wilder than Gilgamesh's subjects, since their heroic nature predisposes them to all sorts of excessive behaviour. The appropriate outlet for such energy is the quest or journey towards a great deed that needs doing. But first Enkidu has to be sufficiently domesticated for this to occur, hence his seduction and initiation into civilisation by Shamhat. She in turn raises other questions, especially with regard to the role of women in epic narratives. She is a crucial intermediary, a representative of civilising behaviour that tames

Enkidu's wildness. And of course this comes at a price; he loses at least some of his strength as a result, allowing Gilgamesh to defeat him in a wrestling bout. Masculine competitive emulation is modulated through a strictly circumscribed femininity. This femininity recurs when the goddess Ishtar tries to seduce Gilgamesh after the two heroes succeed in their quest; this epic will not be the only one to emphasise patriarchal power. Later on in the poem, Siduri, who keeps the inn at the ends of the earth, fails to recognise Gilgamesh as a hero because of his condition after his wanderings; this directly prefigures the *motif* of Odysseus' clandestine return to Ithaca. Utnapishtim's wife operates as a fourth example of a gender politics, and she is not even accorded a name. Ultimately, the return home occurs with Gilgamesh accepting his fate, and becoming content with the everlasting fame he will achieve as the great builder of Uruk. In this respect *Gilgamesh* functions as a foundation narrative.

THE BIBLE

The ways in which the *Atrahasis* anticipates the Old Testament narrative of Noah raises the question of the extent to which the Old Testament can be treated as an 'epic'. The main stumbling-block to perceiving the Old Testament, up to the Second Book of Kings, as an epic, is that it is not explicitly constructed as such. It does not take poetic form, it is composed from multiple disparate elements (books) that are episodic, and covers far too long a time span. Not heroic epic then, but perhaps the epic of a people. It certainly has its fair share of journeys, heroes, kings and supernatural events, not to mention villainous and pure women – all of the elements so familiar from Mesopotamian epics in the mould of the *Atrahasis* or *Gilgamesh*. Stephanie Dalley traces the influence of Babylonian traditions on *Genesis* and *Exodus* in particular (Dalley et al 1998: 64–8). She describes biblical parallels such as the flood story and the importance of triple dreams (Dalley et al 1998: 65–6, 73). She also provides some useful details on scribal training (Dalley et al 1998: 79), reminding us that the assembling of the Old Testament into its familiar form took place in a scribal culture that was saturated with Babylonian practices of scholarship and techniques of presentation.

An overview of the controversy surrounding epic in biblical scholarship is given by Susan Niditch, and she characterises the debate as ranging across the terrain of "national epic material" (Niditch 2009: 277–9). Within this context, it is remarkable that the initial construction of the early books of the Old Testament in particular (the Pentateuch) is often described by analogy with the epic traditions of Mesopotamia and Greece. There are presumed to be oral and written texts that are no longer available to us, but that precede the written versions that have survived. Turning her attention to recent scholarship, Niditch is very careful to place her observations within a field that is broadly encompassed by definitions of epic. Indeed, she gives biblical examples of components that are familiar from other epic traditions: recurring phrases; the role of the hero; war; women; elements of oral performance; and politics. One important distinction is that made between the Pentateuch on the one hand, and the story of the kingdoms of Judea and Israel on the other. Even if the individual critic does not accept that the Pentateuch constitutes an epic in the fullest sense, it is possible for the heroes of later books to be described as falling within the category of epic (Niditch 2009: 282).

Epic episodes would include the story of Samson (Judges 13–16), with its tales of divinely inspired strength and heroism undone by female deception. Heroic combat occurs when David kills Goliath (1 Samuel 17). Solomon dreams of wisdom (1 Kings 3) and is acknowledged as a great builder (1 Kings 5ff). The divinely inspired wild man appears in the guise of Elijah (1 Kings 17ff). Ahab's wife Jezebel reprises the role of the untrustworthy woman, at least in the eyes of the men of religion (1 Kings 19ff). The equivalent of heroic apotheosis occurs with Elijah's whirlwind (2 Kings 2). And of course there is the conquest of Israel by Assyria (2 Kings 18) and that of Judah by Babylon (2 Kings 24). The political story is reprised with a more priestly and scribal gloss in the two books of Chronicles, such that it is tempting to discern hints of an underlying long term conflict between the temporal and spiritual powers in the two kingdoms up to the time of their final destruction. These elements bear comparison with various details that appear in the Greek epics, such as the conflicts between heroes and seers.

Whether or not the Bible should be considered an epic or a series of epic narratives, will ultimately depend on something more than straightforward definitions of what does or does not constitute an epic text. For those who believe in the Bible as a vehicle of truth, it is to be distinguished from the *ethos* of epic in which fictionalised versions of important past events and people who have become semi-legendary are foregrounded. In the Judaeo-Christian traditions, the Bible is elevated beyond epic because it is superior in status. If Genesis is to be taken literally, then the Bible can be seen to adapt elements of epic narrative techniques. However, others might see the Old Testament in particular as simply a variation on a familiar theme (or set of themes) and so could justifiably define it as epic.

GREEK EPIC

Discussions of Greek epic often focus upon the relative merits of Homer and Hesiod, supplemented with a miscellaneous group of shorter texts known as the 'epic cycle'. Stephanie Nelson (among others) notes that the classical Greeks, especially the Athenians, elevated Homer above Hesiod (Nelson 2009: 330). Richard P. Martin analyses this development as part of a wider literary debate. For him, Aristotle's work is the culmination of a trend in literary criticism in which tragedy becomes the privileged form, a yardstick by which all that precedes it is measured. He concludes that: "In short, Homeric poetry is best because it most closely approaches tragic drama" (Martin 2009: 12). Despite what appears to be an anachronism at the core of this argument, there is a certain logic operating here, one that serves as a reminder of the tension between oral communal and literary cultures present in the epics of earlier stages of Greek culture. For Aristotle, following Plato, Athenian tragedy has the status of high culture. All other forms, even the prestigious narratives of Homer and Hesiod, should be judged by comparison with tragedy, a position that is further refined in the Hellenistic age.

In other words, what is beginning to be produced is a hierarchy, with tragedy at its apex. Epic is still highly rated by this sophisticated literary culture, but it is inferior to tragedy. Epic narratives are themselves further subdivided and ranked accordingly: Homer first, Hesiod a close second and other poems from the epic cycle come a distant third (see Davies 1988). This last group comprises a very disparate body of material, and has come down to us via the Aristotelian arrangement of Greek culture:

> [...] the Epic Cycle does not seem to have existed as a unit before the Hellenistic period, though the poems that later were gathered into it stem at least from the Archaic age.
>
> (Burgess 2009: 348)

Burgess provides a useful list of the elements of the cycle (Burgess 2009: 345–6), showing how they fill in many of the gaps left by Homer and Hesiod in representations of heroic legend. He divides the cycle into four broad categories, comprising the early history of the deities, the early and then later wars of Thebes, and stories associated with the Trojan War, especially the so-called *Little Iliad.* Burgess takes great care to differentiate the cycle from other works dealing with myth:

> [...] the Epic Cycle represents a literary manifestation of a long-standing notional arrangement of early Greek myth. But the Epic Cycle is far from comprehensive, and by no means should the Cycle poems be considered the sole or most authoritative narratives of their myth.
>
> (Burgess 2009: 345)

This is an important observation because it emphasises the relative fluidity and incompleteness of the cycle when compared with Hesiod and Homer. The issues raised by Burgess draw attention to the larger discussion of the ways in which Hellenistic elite literary culture constructs its hierarchy of epic texts, a process that had begun several centuries earlier with the rise to prominence of Athenian culture:

> It is clear that as the Homeric poems became more celebrated other, non-Homeric, epic was neglected. The *Iliad* and *Odyssey* were featured at the Panathenaic festival and later became canonical texts at the very center of educational and booktrade circles. The very creation of the Epic Cycle resulted from the marginalization of non-Homeric epic [...]
>
> (Burgess 2009: 350)

Burgess' comments imply that a hegemonic culture is at work in this process. The Greeks differentiated themselves from non-Greek speakers ("Barbarians"), and this process is accelerated and consolidated after the explosion of the Alexandrian Empire from 336 BCE. The Greeks considered themselves to be a superior race, privileging those who spoke Greek over those who did not. The etymology of the term 'barbarism' is 'one who is not a native Greek speaker', a *barbaros*. In this context it is no co-incidence that the classical view of epic, inferior in status to tragedy though it is, is produced by and for a language community that fashioned itself as an elite.

A similar, although less severe, operation is visited upon the works of Hesiod. The differentiation of his *Theogony* and *Works and Days* from the poems of the epic cycle places his poetry on a higher level than those more fragmented poems. Many of the epic cycle's poetry is less well-known to us, but some of them are at least as old as those of Hesiod. The logic by which his work is differentiated from the cycle therefore cannot simply be that of age or authority. Rather, and this is crucial, the separation takes place in terms of literary criteria, particularly those of thematic unity. The same concerns are used in turn to elevate Homer over and above Hesiod:

> A prejudice remains that a tradition cannot create a unified work of art in the way that an individual poet can. The Homeric poems are able to weather this prejudice because their unity lies precisely where we are accustomed to find it, in the narrative. In the Hesiodic case, however, where the unity is one of theme rather than narrative, the less familiar form makes the unity of the poem less apparent to the modern reader.
>
> (Nelson 2009: 331)

In comparison with Homer, Hesiod is represented as more of a didactic poet who utilises the epic form. Nelson describes Hesiod's technique as a "montage" of details (Nelson 2009: 334), using a suggestive term borrowed from film theory. Montage denotes a certain kind of relational difference. It works as an intermediate type between the disorganised multiplicity of a group like the epic cycle poems on the one hand, and the much more structurally unified narratives of Homeric epic on the other. Montage has its own relatively organised arrangements, albeit in a less stringently formal sense than those attributed to poems such as the *Iliad*. Furthermore, in his Introduction to Hesiod's poems, M.L. West notes some points of comparison with debates around the constitution of the Bible as epic, especially since the issue of the Bible as 'epic' might be related to its relatively episodic nature (in Hesiod 1988: xix).

Interestingly, West also recognises the literary categories produced by the Greeks, following Plato, when he describes the mythological roots of the succession myth in Hesiod's *Theogony*:

> It is a story of crude and bizarre acts of violence, of gods castrating, swallowing, and generally clobbering each other in a way that sophisticated readers of Plato's time found strange and unacceptable. We now know that it was not the product of Hesiod's savage fantasy, but a Hellenized version of an oriental myth [...].
>
> (West in Hesiod 1988: xi–xii)

This is a timely reminder of the fact that Hesiod (or whoever wrote down the poems attributed to him) was not writing for the literate readers of Plato's Athens. Once again, it must be emphasised that these earlier poems were produced for an oral tradition well before they were reorganised within the parameters of a literary cultural elite.

At the height of the Greek epic stands the dual monolith of the *Iliad* and the *Odyssey*. Just as West notes the correspondences between Hesiod's poetry and Near Eastern mythology, Walter Burkert sees the typology of the divine that operates in the *Iliad* in particular as just one instance of a series of patternings that can be traced back to the *Atrahasis* (Burkert 2009: 298–9).

Modern readers find it rather surprising that many of the most notable incidents from the Trojan War are absent from the poem, particularly the narrative of the Greek deception of the wooden horse. The *Iliad* is instead a much more tightly woven narrative sequence that traverses a short period in the war, the consequences of Achilles' feud with Agamemnon. But even the death of Achilles does not occur in the *Iliad*. Instead, the poem uses techniques of foreshadowing to convey a sense of impending events that lie outwith the poem itself, but are well enough known to the epic's audiences to be understood. It is precisely this relatively tightly woven narrative structure that informs the later literary judgement of the poem, even if it is remembered that the poem is not necessarily the product of a single imagination. Gaps in the sequence of events are filled in by some elements of the epic cycle discussed above, and also by the much later figure of Quintus of Smyrna (James 2007).

In many ways the Hellenistic view is often replicated by later critics and editors. The editor of the Penguin Classics edition of the *Iliad*, Martin Hammond, begins his Introduction with an acknowledgement of the importance of the oral tradition that lies behind the Homeric texts as we have them (in Homer 1987: viii). However, during his discussion of the oral tradition and Homer, Hammond feels the need to compare Homeric epic to tragedy. He writes that "[...] the *Iliad* is the first, and greatest, of the Greek tragedies" (Hammond in Homer 1987: xiii). He goes on to give a very useful critical summary of the poem (from xviii–l), but even here the need to refer to tragedy resurfaces. Agamemnon is described as a "stage-tyrant" (xix), and the relationship between Hector and Paris is described within a tragic context (xxv). When it comes to the vexed question of the relationship between the *Iliad* and the *Odyssey*, Hammond states that "The *Iliad* is a tragedy, the *Odyssey* a romance" (xvii).

In his Introduction to Robert Fagles' translation of the *Odyssey* (Homer 1996), Bernard Knox refers to Shakespeare by analogy when he describes the Cyclops Polyphemus as "[...] a demonized version of the native, like Shakespeare's Caliban" (Knox 1996: 27). Two related issues emerge from such a problematic comparison. The first is the ease with which two radically different texts from distant epochs are yoked together. And the second is the way in which it is assumed that the reader of this Introduction to the *Odyssey* will already know who Caliban is; the reference is not explained in the text itself, other than by mentioning Shakespeare's name. Knox repeats the procedure elsewhere when he describes Odysseus' visit to the underworld:

> It is a vision that has echoed down the centuries, that lies behind Propertius' magical line *sunt apud infernos tot milia formasorum* – "so many thousands of lovely women among the dead – and Campion's "shades of underground ... White Iope, blithe Helen, and the rest".
>
> (Knox 1996: 50)

It is assumed that the reader will know who Propertius and Campion are; but at least the critic translates the Latin in a vaguely limpid gesture towards a wider reading public. Here the modern critic subsumes genres into a comparative discussion of literary taste in an *ethos* where certain texts have come to occupy a canonical status. The same assumptions lie behind Fagles' notes on the spelling and pronunciation of Homeric names: "[...] we have thought it best to work with pronunciation that Keats and Shelley would have recognized" (Fagles in Homer 1996: 66). The reference to Romantic poets from nearly 200 years ago is revealing: why not Derek Walcott?

Despite its saturation in the traditional discourses of liberal humanist criticism, Knox's Introduction to the *Odyssey* includes an excellent section on the historical importance of oral culture to the *Iliad* and the *Odyssey*, in his description of Milman Parry's work on epic orality (Knox 1996: 14–17; see Parry 1988). This leads in turn to a fruitful discussion of the relationship between orality and writing in the construction of these particular texts, especially the use of the epic epithet as a metrical device (Knox 1996: 18–22). Thus, while Knox's introduction repeats the assumptions of other literary criticism, he also takes on board the historical context of the reception of early epic by audiences steeped in the assumptions of an oral culture. The result is an uneasy exposition that switches between two discursive frameworks. This demonstrates that epic texts are never represented innocently; the critical perspective always attempts, even if unconsciously, to inform the exposition presented to its readers.

Issues such as these extend beyond the work of any single writer, and the effects will be found symptomatically in the commentary and translator's critical vocabulary. Richard Hamilton Armstrong gives some examples of the latter when he discusses the translations of Chapman and Pope (Armstrong 2009: 179–82). He notes the occurrence of terms that are either mistranslated or even interpolated in order to bring the Homeric texts fully into line with the values of the English upper classes during the rise and expansion of the British Empire. It becomes impossible therefore to separate out completely a given classical epic from its reproduction and consumption by later cultures. In fact, there is no such thing as 'epic', simply stated: it is always and inevitably imbricated in a host of assumptions about the cultural capital of the Western classics. The examples from Knox and Armstrong demonstrate that Homer is particularly open to various kinds of appropriation, as Western culture seeks to divorce the poems from their oral communal roots and set them on a pedestal.

Elements of the *Iliad* and the *Odyssey* which are open to appropriation as literature can be broadly categorised under the headings of fame, warfare, and the return home. War is really a subset of fame (*kleos* in Greek), because it is often the main arena within which glorious undying fame is won. The homecoming (*nostos*) is somewhat more complex because it presents a different set of problems for the hero to overcome, and is bound up with relations between guests and hosts. It is probably sufficient to state at this point that the *Iliad* is mostly associated with fame, and the *Odyssey* with homecoming, since these are the themes that influence the poetry that comes after them as part of a process of canon formation.

A case in point is the *Argonautica* by Apollonius of Rhodes (c. 260 BCE). This poem is concerned with the generation of semi-divine heroes that predates the events of the Trojan War and its immediate aftermath. Apollonius models his story of the voyage of the *Argo* very much on the *Odyssey*, but he also takes advantage of the kinship relations between his heroes and their successors to foreshadow the events of the Trojan War, in the process replicating many of the techniques found in the *Iliad*. The relationship between his composition and the two Homeric poems enables Apollonius to demonstrate his mastery of the epic, in a manner that modern literary theory recognises as intertextual. This is no coincidence, since Apollonius was curator of the great library of the Ptolemaic dynasty, one of the houses vying for power as a successor to Alexander of Macedon. This poet-curator is placed right at the heart of the Hellenistic establishment and so is well able to construct a poem that resonates with associations of its predecessors. For a full recounting of the narrative, see Nelis (2009: 355–6), who also emphasises the ways in which the poem engages with the literary tastes prevalent at the time of its writing.

The Greek of the *Argonautica* is deliberately archaic, as Richard Hunter notes in his edition of the poem:

> I have tried to convey both the stylistic variety of the poem, and the fact that all of it is written in a language very far from the everyday.
> (Hunter in Apollonius of Rhodes 2009: Preface)

Apollonius couches the literary style of his poem in such a way that it establishes a direct intertextual contact with its Homeric predecessors, in a kind of linguistic undercurrent. But this is not just an academic exercise in historical recovery divorced from the real contemporary world of the poet:

> The very subject of Apollonius' epic, a voyage to distant lands and strange peoples (cf. Alexander's Eastern conquests), bringing the Argonauts into contact with areas of considerable political interest to the Ptolemies (the Black Sea, Cyrenaica, the Aegean islands), gives this poem a contemporary dimension which should not be overlooked; too often the 'Alexandrian-ness' of the *Argonautica* has been seen merely in the apparatus of scholarly learning which the poem displays.
> (Hunter in Apollonius of Rhodes 2009: xi)

Apollonius is, therefore, writing an epic for a very specific readership and his poem is driven by a precise rationale. So much so, indeed, that it becomes very difficult to separate epic out from its uses in the culture of the time. Hunter goes on in his introduction to emphasise the relationship between the poem and the community for which it was intended (in Apollonius of Rhodes 2009: xii–xiii). However, he also draws attention to the self-referential nature of the exercise of writing itself in the Hellenistic period:

[...] there is also in Alexandrian poetry an extreme self-consciousness, an overt sense of itself as poetry, and a constant willingness to comment upon itself and its function.

(Hunter in Apollonius of Rhodes 2009: xiii)

Apollonius finds in the Homeric poems a relatively unified narrative. He extends and refines what he finds in such a way that his poem comments not only upon the Homeric texts and its Alexandrian present, but also upon its own literary status as well. The technique used to effect this is that of a narrative persona who has a distinctive 'voice':

Thus, a very noticeable feature of the *Argonautica*, particularly in comparison to the Homeric poems, is how often the narrator speaks 'in his own voice' to comment upon the events of the story.

(Hunter in Apollonius of Rhodes 2009: xiv)

Thus, the logic of artistic unity emphasised in Greek culture is here taken even further by means of what, to a modern audience, is a clearly literary narrative technique. It is hard to imagine a recitation of *Gilgamesh* to a contemporary audience that privileges the identity of an omniscient speaker in this way.

Characterisation is another major aspect that undergoes modification in the *Argonautica*. This is important because it is through action that heroic characters achieve their glory and fame. Following on from the *Iliad* and the *Odyssey* it is possible to discern, at least provisionally, two major elements that pertain to heroic character in action. These are the outright forcefulness in war that is crucial before the walls of Troy and also the subtlety of strategic and tactical planning, which includes the trickery practised by Odysseus. The second may well be less glorious than the first in and of itself, but it is necessary before Odysseus can return home. The *Argonautica* refines and develops the differentiation between these two elements of the hero. For example, Jason never succeeds at anything without outside help; it comes either from interested divinities, because he is destined to succeed in his quest and return home, or from other characters, especially Medea. Noble heroism in this poem is therefore achieved by less obviously noble means than through the warfare of the *Iliad*, since in the case of Jason it is conferred upon him by others; it is not intrinsic to him in the way it is for figures such as Achilles. Jason is not the kind of hero who would choose a short life filled with glory over a long life of anonymous peace. The point is underscored in the way that the poem has Herakles begin the voyage, but then removes him part way through, because he is presumably far too heroic in comparison with Jason. As a son of Zeus, father and king of the gods, Herakles is the greatest of all the heroes. The Hellenistic characterisation of the heroic is thus inflected with other emphases that take the narrative in a different direction.

There is a further doubling of equivocation in the way this poem presents its heroes, and it too can be traced to the effects of Greek and Hellenistic culture. Almost all of the *Argonautica*'s intended readership knew their literature very well indeed, including plays such as the *Medea* (Euripides 2002). A kind of intertextual dramatic irony is produced when such a reader already has knowledge of the later events of Jason and Medea's relationship, as well as Jason's rather inglorious death. He betrays Medea, she leaves him, and he becomes an alcoholic. He has one too many drinks, falls asleep inside the shell of the *Argo*, and is killed when pieces of it (including the divine component) fall on his head during a storm. Such a context inevitably undermines Jason's heroic status. Additionally, as D.P. Nelis realises (2009: 362), the powerful presence of Medea presents another set of problems. The poem represents her in different ways at different times, depending on the needs of the narrative. This leads to elements of inconsistency as she goes from being a helpless victim of Eros at first sight of Jason to an extremely powerful sorceress; she even helps Jason to murder her own brother.

The culture to which this poem belongs is able to accommodate heroic intertextual references, but the result is that it does not produce its own great heroic figures. The deeds of heroes whose lineage is divine accords much more closely with those of normal humans and as a result the world they are shown to inhabit appears less elevated. The complex relativism that results from this secularisation seems to suit later poets writing in Greek as well. The *Dionysiaca* of Nonnos takes the logic even further, with Dionysus managing most of his conquests, especially his sexual ones, with the aid of his invention of wine. This little-known work dates from very late antiquity, and the most accessible text is provided in the Loeb Classical Library (Nonnos 1989). Overall, it can be said that as the literary tradition of works written in Greek develops and matures, the influence of the earliest classical models becomes dispersed and to some extent interrogated.

LATIN EPIC

The first major Roman epic is the *Annales* of Ennius, of which only fragments remain (Ennius 1989, also in the Loeb Classical Library). The title suggests that its narrative is organised according to an annual cycle, which is consistent with the Roman state calendric system of dating by consular terms of office. Another major early text is the *Bellum Poenicum* of Naevius, which again survives only in fragments, although enough does remain for a putative reconstruction to be made, and to give a flavour of its style and contents (Naevius 1989 in the Loeb Classical Library). The most important point to be made is that the *Bellum Poenicum* demonstrates a Roman concern with what has often been called secondary, or historical epic. Its subject is the conflict between Rome and Carthage over the island of Sicily, the war we know as the First Punic War. It is also possible that later lost books dealt with Hannibal's invasion of Italy. Susan M. Goldberg provides a useful overview of our knowledge of early Latin epic in an essay in Foley's edited collection (Goldberg 2009). She shows how

Naevius developed the techniques of epic writing from his predecessor, Livius Andronicus, who wrote Latin epics in the metre
known as the 'Saturnian', because its archaic form is not entirely
understood. Andronicus wrote just before and during the great
war against Hannibal's Carthage, which culminated in the Roman
victory of Zama in 202 BCE. Andronicus chose as his epic subject
matter the wanderings of Odysseus and was also a dramatist.
Naevius shifted the emerging Latin epic tradition into more
familiar historical terrain.

The relationship that Naevius established between epic and
history is crucial to later Roman epic narratives, for two very
important reasons. The first, and perhaps more obvious, is the
relatively late arrival of Latin as a major literary language when
compared with Greek. So many Greek epic and mythic narratives
existed prior to the rise of the Roman Republic that it took
centuries for Latin to develop as a language to the point where
it could compete with Greek. Second is the crucial historical
context of the consolidation of the Republic and the development
of empire, including the civil wars that culminated in the establishment of the Principate by Augustus. It is no mere accident
that the Latin language begins to produce its major epics from
this point in Roman history. The result is that Roman epic is
indelibly marked by empire in a way that is absent from the
relatively fragmented Greek polities, or the competing Successor
dynasties.

It is the Roman drive to *imperium* that provides the context
for Virgil's *Aeneid* although, as Jenkyns observes, Virgil owes a
literary debt to one of his immediate predecessors, Lucretius:

> The Nature of Things showed Virgil the way to the Georgics, and the
> Georgics showed him that he could attempt an even longer poem,
> his epic Aeneid.
>
> (Jenkyns 2007: xxii)

Jenkyns describes how Lucretius provides the didactic framework
for Virgil's epic in an intertextual relationship that recalls the
double strand of Hesiod and Homer. The result is a lasting
influence on conceptions of the poet in the Western tradition: the

notion of the poetic career that strives upwards through mastery of lesser literary forms to the epic as the most prestigious genre (compare Spenser or Milton, for example). In the immediate context of the late Roman Republic, another point needs to be stressed: with Lucretius Roman literary culture for the first time appropriates and extends what is originally a Greek poetic form.

The example of Lucretius provides Virgil with the linguistic confidence to proceed with his own project, although he has a different set of priorities comparatively speaking from those of the *Argonautica* of Apollonius of Rhodes. The structure of the *Aeneid* parallels the two Homeric epics, with the *Odyssey* serving as the model for the first six books, and the *Iliad* for books seven to twelve. This demonstrates Virgil's mastery of the formal requirements for writing epic. In terms of content, he weaves together several disparate strands of legend to produce a foundation myth in epic form. He appropriates the figure of Aeneas of Troy as the ultimate progenitor of what will become the Roman state, and indulges in some rather dubious uses of the mythology of the *Julii*, the dynasty of Julius Caesar and Augustus. The *Julii* claim descent from Ascanius, the son of Aeneas, who is renamed Iulus when the Trojan survivors set up their new state in Italy. Aeneas himself is a son of Venus, which provides the important divine connection to a heroic bloodline. One of the main actions undertaken by Julius Caesar in Rome was the rebuilding of an old temple to Venus, which ensured that from then on his family name would always be linked in the popular imagination with the goddess.

Of course, this sleight of hand is ready-made for Virgil. The triumph of Aeneas explicitly prefigures the moment at which Virgil produces his work, when the dynasty of Aeneas returns to supreme power at the head of a new empire. The sense of closure that is produced is very powerful. It helps to explain the supremacy of Virgil's work in Latin and beyond into the Middle Ages. Craig Kallendorf explains how during the period of relative scarcity of Greek texts, Virgil's *Aeneid* becomes the superlative example of the epic form (Kallendorf 2009). However, the case for Virgil as a poet who celebrates empire is compromised by the ambivalent ending of the poem. When the unruly native champion Turnus is wounded and defeated in heroic single combat by Aeneas, he pleads for his life. In a fit of fury, the Trojan kills him because he sees the Italian wearing the baldric he took from one of his own previous victims, Aeneas' ally Pallas. Empire is established at a very violent price, as David Quint realises in his treatment of the killing of Turnus:

> His victory over Turnus is a vindication both for himself and for his defeated Trojan nation.
>
> This vindication and the reciprocity of doing unto others what has been done to oneself amount to a taking of vengeance upon the past.
>
> (Quint 1993: 74–5)

Quint relates the death of Turnus to a logic of reciprocal repetition that links the *Aeneid* to its Homeric antecedents. Just as Diomedes and Odysseus kill Dolon in the *Iliad*, so too Turnus kills the son of Dolon. The wheel finally comes full circle when Turnus meets his death at the hands of Aeneas. This is not just personal vengeance; it is the revenge of an entire nation. The death of Turnus is therefore an emblematic moment. It brings together meanings from the epic tradition, the Roman foundation myth, and the re-founding of Rome under Augustus.

The poem's concern with empire is sustained throughout, so much so that the *Aeneid* is full of elements that relate directly to Roman history. The cyclical return to the descendants of Aeneas demonstrates this conclusively, while the poet's concern with the Roman past could be said to be the poem's main structuring principle. In the introduction to his edition of the *Aeneid*, C. Day Lewis pinpoints the complex timeline that Virgil employs:

> A hundred years of decline and disorder was addressed at last: that might count as a second foundation of the city, and present Augustus as another Aeneas, another god-sent deliverer. Such a conception was much better presented in the form of prophetic utterances and visions of the future than in narrative about a central actor in the story, and that is how, in the *Aeneid*, Augustus is presented.
>
> (Virgil 2008: xviii)

Since Aeneas functions in the poem as so much more than an epic hero, he is made to embody the concept of *pietas* that is so fundamental to Rome's understanding of its place in the world, as Lewis notes (in Virgil 2008: xxii). The idea encompasses the willing subjection of the self to service to greater powers, including the state, and it underwrites the relationship between Aeneas and his imperial destiny. The overarching sense of submission to a national destiny forces Aeneas to break off his relationship with Dido, the mythical Queen of Carthage. This in turn leads her to curse Aeneas and his people as she immolates herself, furnishing a mythical origin for the historical conflict between Rome and Carthage. Empire is thus underwritten by *pietas*.

By contrast with Virgil's resolutely Roman epic, Ovid's *Metamorphoses* (8 CE) challenges conceptions of epic that depend on definitions of form. Carole E. Newlands has observed that:

> The *Metamorphoses* is not an anthology of myth (although often, even today, it is treated as such), for Ovid audaciously and ingeniously connects the myths to one another in a variety of ways to create a smooth, if artificial temporal progression.
>
> (Newlands 2009: 477)

In this way, Ovid's text has had an important intertextual history, especially via Golding's Elizabethan translation, since it becomes a repository of *motifs* for Renaissance English writers such as Shakespeare and many others. The effects produced by Ovid's individual mythemes can obviously be traced in turn to Lucretius, although the two poets treat religion and myth entirely differently. Lucretius is a strict materialist, basing his conception of the universe on the Epicurean model:

> On the largest and the smallest scale there is immutability: the universe is the sum of infinite space and an infinite number of atoms, and nothing can be added to it or subtracted from it; and each single atom is immortal, indivisible and indestructible. In between, everything is activity and mutability, for the atoms are in ceaseless

energetic motion. The drama lies in this combination of change and
changelessness [...]

(Jenkyns 2007: xii)

The philosophical underpinnings here could not be more different
from Ovid's. For Lucretius the gods do exist, but are of a
different order of being from humans, and therefore have abso-
lutely no interest in humanity (Lucretius 2007: 209), while Ovid
of course relishes stories of divine interference in human affairs.
The one thing the two poets do have in common is a fundamental
interest in the logic of change, and in this respect Ovid owes a
great deal to his predecessor.

Many of the mythical vignettes related by Ovid have become
particularly famous. Episodes that come into this category
would include, for example, the transformation of Actaeon
(Book 3); the story of Echo and Narcissus (Book 3); Pyramus
and Thisbe (Book 4); Hermaphroditus (Book 4); Arachne
(Book 5); the death of Icarus (Book 8); Hyacinthus (Book 10);
Pygmalion (Book 10); Venus and Adonis (Book 10); and the
golden touch of Midas (Book 11). However, as Newlands points
out, there is nevertheless an overarching temporal movement in
the text as it is organised. Ovid delineates an overall progression
through generations of Greek personages that culminates in a
return to history with the emergence of Rome. In order to do
so, Ovid produces a structure based on narrative patterning.
Major mythic events and heroic deeds form the main thrust
of the developing timeline, with various shorter stories providing relief.

When he reaches the fall of Troy and then the flight of
Aeneas in Books 12 and 13, Ovid moves into the same territory
as Virgil. He even covers ground that does not appear at all
in Virgil's version. Instead of foreshadowing the emergence
of Augustus, Ovid treats of Aeneas' apotheosis and relates the
history of his successors up to and including the apotheosis of
Romulus, which ends Book 14. The poem's final book includes a
long description of the teachings of Pythagoras, and the emphasis
here upon the importance of change has much in common with
Lucretius:

In all the world there is not that that standeth at a stay.
Things ebb and flow, and every shape is made to pass away.
The time itself continually is fleeting like a brook,
For neither brook nor lightsome time can tarry still.

(Ovid 2002: 441)

This is the immediate context for Ovid's tracing of the remainder of Roman history up to his own day, including the *apotheosis* of Julius Caesar and the destiny of Augustus, which will create yet another Roman divinity. Ovid's poem finishes as a pagan teleology; the hymn to change inscribes the emerging history of the Roman state with a certain inevitability, making Rome the successor to the myths and history of Greece. The Roman poet sets the seal on his version of the imperial triumph by noting the divinity of his story's major heroes. The poem's move into history is in contrast silent on the achievements of Hellenistic personages such as Alexander of Macedon.

However, nothing about Ovid is straightforward. As he writes this Roman ending upon Greek mythology, it is possible to detect a suppressed snigger at the expense of Caesar and his successor, Augustus. As David Quint points out:

Ovid is not above irony, and his narrator has earlier declared with a straight face that Caesar had to be killed and made into a god in order that his son would not be born of mortal seed.

(Quint 1993: 77)

The point being, of course, that Octavian (who later becomes Augustus) is not of Caesar's seed, being an adopted great-nephew. Alternatives are registered to the epic worldview of empire.

Poets of the next few generations into the early Empire period continue with the relationship between epic and history. They do so, however, in a set of very changed circumstances that is comprised of two important strands. The first is political, involving the necessity and difficulty of writing in the times of the emperors. The second is literary, reflecting the intertextual shadows cast by the *Aeneid*. The career of Lucan is particularly emblematic of this double problem because it leads to his own death. Initially he is a favourite of Nero's, probably due to a combination of Lucan's personal charisma and family connections – his uncle is Nero's tutor Seneca. Lucan falls into disfavour with Nero and then becomes embroiled in one of the plots against the emperor, as a result of which he has to take his own life at the age of 26.

Named after the famous battle in which Julius Caesar's defeated Pompey, Lucan's *Pharsalia* is also often entitled *Bellum Civile*, which is a more accurate rendering of the poem's subject matter. Although the Battle of Pharsalus is a major climactic moment in the poem, the narrative continues to describe many of the events subsequent to the battle itself. The effect is subtly to undercut reader expectations of a major finishing point similar to that of the *Aeneid*; Lucan is of course indebted to the earlier epic, but he also plays with the form. David Quint makes some initial observations on Lucan's relationship with Virgil in the introduction to his book *Epic and Empire* (Quint 1993: 5–8), where he notes that the *Pharsalia* does not simply replicate Virgil's techniques, but constitutes an intertextual engagement with the relationship between epic and empire. He describes the crucial intervention made by the *Aeneid*:

> The *Aeneid* had, in fact, decisively transformed epic for posterity into both a genre that was committed to imitating and attempting to 'overgo' its earlier versions and a genre that was overtly political: Virgil's epic is tied to a specific national history, to the idea of world domination, to a monarchical system, even to a particular dynasty.
>
> (Quint 1993: 8)

This is an extremely important observation for the literary history of the epic subsequent to Virgil. It bifurcates the genre along parallel lines. The first, the attempt to improve upon and surpass previous works, is stylistic and technical. The second is resolutely political. The two come together in the *Aeneid* most powerfully, resonating through subsequent centuries. Quint borrows the term "epic continuity" from Thomas M. Greene (Quint 1993: 369, n.14) and suggests that this combination of form and content has to be addressed by writers such as Lucan, even as they attempt to react against it:

> Lucan, as if prescient of a literary history that would last two millennia after him, correctly identifies and blames Virgil for this continuity – and for the continuity of an ideology of empire that a henceforth Virgilian epic tradition would encode and transmit.
>
> (Quint 1993: 8)

As a later victim of exactly the dynasty the *Aeneid* praises, Lucan is well aware of the uses to which the Virgilian ideology of empire can be put. This is the reason for the relative absence of divine power in Lucan (discussed by Quint 1993: 133). It also explains why the later poet spreads wide the net of his literary knowledge in order to undercut the power of the earlier epic. His depiction of Caesar includes a very specific reference to Caesar's own writing techniques when he makes the general speak of himself in the third person:

> Now Rubicon is passed, no stream on earth
> Shall hinder Caesar!
>
> (Lucan 2008: 35)

Lucan makes Caesar continually speak in this way in order to represent himself as heroic, a particularly effective variation on the story within a story (another example can be found at Lucan 2008: 48). However, just because Caesar sees himself as a great hero does not necessarily mean that everyone else does. Lucan's narrative treads a very thin line between glorification and outright condemnation:

> Such a triumph had he lost
> By further conquest.
>
> (Lucan 2008: 47)

This is a very precise rendering of the consequences of Caesar starting the civil war. The former triumvir is unable to receive the triumph he deserves in Rome for his previous conquests because he is now directly embroiled in conflict with other Romans. The technique is particularly clever, almost questioning Caesar by oblique implication. It is probably the best way for Lucan to deal with the loss of liberty entailed by the rise of the empire without directly challenging the rule of the Caesars. Lucan maintains his precarious balance by not making Caesar's cause seem more just than that of his competitors until the Republican troops break a sacred truce (Lucan 2008: 73). Even so, this is balanced out by making a direct rhetorical question to Caesar (145):

> Didst favour gain
> By sacrifice in this thine impious war?

This is how Sir Edward Ridley translated the line in his edition of the poem published in 1896. His conventional use of heightened poetic diction demonstrates the underlying issues at stake in Lucan's representation: Caesar was the *pontifex maximus*, chief priest of the Roman state religion, but by asking if his war is "impious", Lucan implicitly challenges the Caesarean interpretation. Indeed, he reinforces his point by making the dying Pompey speak to foreshadow Caesar's own death (Lucan 2008: 157), linking the Roman pair intertextually with Achilles and Hector. In a similar manner, Lucan makes use of events in Greece to showcase his knowledge of the Greek myths (126).

The text often undercuts itself in this way, sometimes managing its material by inverting normal epic patterns. Instead of praising the greater deeds of the heroes of antiquity, historically recent Romans are shown to surpass them, as with the reference to Parthia (116). In Book 9, Cato's troops are shown to wander the deserts of North Africa in even greater suffering than that of the Argonauts. The final book uses a displacement technique to make an anti-war (and anti-conquest) statement when it describes the damage wrought by Alexander of Macedon (226–7). Even so, as David Quint points out (Quint 1993: 156–7), Lucan has no problem with the imperial glory of Rome. His quarrel is with the principate that has appropriated rule of the empire for a monarchy.

As Shadi Bartsch realises, many of Lucan's sentiments, and the stylistic exposition of them, do not necessarily find favour with his contemporaries (Bartsch 2009). However, Lucan does develop in epic form many of the techniques and intertextual references that become staples for those who follow him. One of the most conventional, perhaps, is Valerius Flaccus, whose *Argonautica* is deeply indebted to Apollonius of Rhodes. The Harvard Loeb Classical Library edition of 1936 includes an introduction by J.H. Mozley that goes some way to delineating this particular poem's conventionality. However, Flaccus does demonstrate some moments of originality, for example when he includes the death of Jason's father Aeson, which does not occur in Ovid (Mozley 1936: x). Mozley also shows how Flaccus is at variance with Apollonius (xii). Flaccus may well have made his changes to the legend to demonstrate his knowledge of various mythic elements, some of which do in fact contradict one another. Even so, Andrew Zissos argues that:

> While his debt to Apollonius is clearly substantial, Valerius operates principally on a schematic level: his treatment of the episodes themselves is invariably innovative.

> (Zissos 2009: 506)

What is not in doubt is the stylistic debt Flaccus owes to Virgil (Mozley 1936: xv; Zissos 2009: 508). The eight books of the poem that have survived indicate that it is incomplete, so it is difficult to tell whether or not the poem would have continued in this vein in its finished state. Nevertheless, as a so-called 'silver' Latin poem in comparison with the 'golden age' of Augustan poetry, it demonstrates many of the ways in which Roman writers continue to inhabit and develop the epic.

A direct contemporary of Flaccus is Publius Papinius Statius, writer of a Latin version of the story of the seven against Thebes, *The Thebaid* (Statius 2004). This story is well known in antiquity, and there is a Greek version in the Epic cycle, which has not survived. Unlike the relationship between the *Argonautica* of Flaccus and that of Apollonius, it is therefore impossible to say with any certainty how indebted Statius is to his Greek predecessor. Unlike the case of Flaccus, *The Thebaid* is complete. It recounts the story of the first group of seven heroes to attack Thebes in the period just before the Trojan War. There are the usual structural and thematic parallels with previous epics, especially *The Iliad*, but Statius implicitly criticises the ways in which his heroes behave in the conflict. In this he has a great deal in common with Lucan.

The war that takes place in *The Thebaid* comes about when the rule of Thebes falls to the brothers Eteocles and Polynices, sons of Oedipus and Jocasta. It is agreed that they shall divide the rulership between them in alternating five-year periods, and Eteocles wins the first session by lot. He then refuses to give it up, and *The Thebaid* details the ensuing conflict. The crucial importance of fratricidal conflict has obvious resonances for the Roman poet, and Statius makes the parallels with recent Roman history explicit in his invocation to the muse at the start of Book 1 (Statius 2004: 1–2). The theme of civil war ignites a whole series of signifiers of Roman practices. For example, the convocation of the gods is translated into a secular equivalent as a meeting of the Senate under the Emperor (8ff). Statius makes a partial invocation to Mithras (26), a deity that achieved prominence well after the events at Thebes. Roman military terms are used to make the action seem contemporary to the reader: heavy javelins (*pila*, 86); legions (106); and cohorts (213). Macedonian pikemen similar to those of Alexander the Great appear (185), and the Etruscan roots of Roman augury are mentioned (78). These instances are not simply anachronistic, with that term's implications of error. Rather, *The Thebaid* uses Roman *motifs* to emplot the Theban conflict retrospectively as a Roman conflict. The interplay of meaning between the past and present re-inscribes the Greek story within recent Roman history, a process of interweaving rather than straightforward anachronism. The resultant secularisation of the narrative implies that the gods are not entirely the direct causes of the action, making the human personages much more responsible for their choices and deeds.

Of course, Statius knows exactly what he is doing here. His work is very self-conscious about its place in a mature Roman epic tradition. It follows Virgil in its delaying of the inevitable conflict at Thebes by six of the 12 books, a very precise parallel with the *Aeneid*. Book 12 is entitled *Clementia*, which is supposedly one of the main virtues of the Caesars. However, clemency is only provisionally reinstated at Thebes by the intrusion of Theseus from Athens. In one respect he functions as a kind of Augustus figure. However, such a move is always going to be ambivalent in Roman writing after Ovid and, especially, following Lucan. Many of Statius' readers would know that another seven heroes will mass against Thebes after the events of this war. Since Statius is writing under the Empire, he has to maintain a careful balance between registering the woeful effects of civil war on the one hand, and the example of Lucan on the other. *The Thebaid* is unable fully to criticise recent Roman leaders, so Statius displaces his concerns very precisely onto a mythical Theban past.

The poet uses two main literary techniques in order to smooth out this particular operation. The first, adapted from Ovid, is the use of the story within the story. The first occurrence comes early on when King Adrastus of Argos is awoken by fighting outside his front door. Having fled from Thebes, Polynices has just encountered another suppliant, Tydeus, and the two of them indulge in a furious bout of unarmed combat. Adrastus breaks them apart and then tells the story of Apollo slaying the Python. This section of the poem is important because it brings together very quickly three of the main heroes who will lead the force against Thebes, and it does so in a setting of extreme violence at the entrance to the king's house. It also immediately sets up the narration of divine violence. This is all very reminiscent of Ovid's *Metamorphoses*, and indeed Statius makes an explicit reference to the title and contents of the earlier poem:

> Sacred it stood, divine with age. They say
> Not only ancestors of men, but nymphs
> And flocks of fauns dwelled there in olden days.
> The metamorphosed ones remained, but ruin
> And misery now overcame the forest.

(Statius 2004: 144)

The involvement of the divine has important consequences, because the other four heroes are all marked in some way by a relationship with the gods. Amphiaraus has been gifted with the foresight of the inspired seer by Apollo. He is killed during the combat at Thebes when the ground opens up to swallow him and his chariot whole. Capaneus functions as his exact opposite; although he is a great warrior, he is also an out-and-out atheist. He is killed by Jupiter's thunderbolts as he scales the walls of the city. The powerful fighter Hippomedon is overwhelmed by the waters of the River Ismenus outside Thebes and dispatched by the enemy once he has lost his strength. The seventh, Parthenopaeus, is still young and dies fighting. He is the son of the famous warrior servant of Diana, Atalanta. Tydeus himself is killed when beset by many enemies, gnawing in his fury at the head of his slain counterpart, and Polynices and Eteocles kill each other in single combat. Only Adrastus survives. William J. Dominik provides a useful commentary on the uses and abuses of the supernatural in the poem (Dominik 2009: 519–20). He shows how this catalogue of brutality relates in multiple ways to the gods, a very subtle rendering of the divine claims of various claimants to the Roman Empire.

The second internal story is that of Hypsipyle in Book 5. Her appearance in the poem links the seven heroes with the story of Jason, since he and Hypsipyle had been lovers. As with the references to divinity, this is hardly a positive correspondence. Hypsipyle has been abducted by raiders after Jason abandoned her, although she is later reunited with their two children.

The second main literary technique Statius uses to underpin his narrative comes when he personifies abstract qualities as minor deities in their own right:

> The radiance of Phoebus
> Weakens on contact with this seat of Mars;
> It makes the light afraid, and its hard gleam
> saddens the stars. The posted guards befit it:
> mad-moving Haste, who leaps through outer gates,
> blind Wickedness, pale Fear, and blood-red Rage.

> (Statius 2004: 177)

Other examples of such allegorising can be found at Statius 2004: 267 and 287. Book 11 is entitled *Pietas*, which twins with *Clementia* to produce the main elements of Caesarean (and Augustan) ideology. This particular aspect will go on to have great influence on the development of medieval and then Renaissance epics, with their insistence on the importance of allegory. In the introduction to his edition of the poem, Charles Stanley Ross traces the implications of allegory and Statius' influence on later poems (in Statius 2004: ix). Indeed, he goes so far as to declare *The Thebaid* "the last successful epic written in Rome" (xvi). Of course, its relative success may be attributed to the fact that the poem is complete as well as fully embedded in the silver Latin epic tradition. This differentiates it from incomplete contemporary works such as that of Valerius Flaccus, or the *Punica* of Silius Italicus. The precise historical and cultural location of *The Thebaid* also marks it off from much later works such as those of Claudian, whose works seem to be pushing against the boundaries of what is permissible in epic composition. Michael H. Barnes describes Claudian's career as an apologist for the general Stilicho in the years before the fall of Rome to the Goths in 410 CE (Barnes 2009), situating Claudian at the edge of the shift from antiquity to the post-Roman world of the so-called Middle Ages. Claudian's historically liminal position leads Barnes to claim that:

> Amidst all this variation and innovation, we must recognize in the end that the meaning of epic is, finally, whatever the culture in which it is embedded decides that it is.
>
> (Barnes 2009: 545)

This is an important observation, since it postulates a fluidity and dynamism to the epic function, one that should be remembered when dealing with later epic works as well as those produced by radically different cultures from those of the Western European tradition.

THE SANSKRIT EPICS

The two main Sanskrit epics, the *Mahabharata* and the *Ramayana* are slowly becoming better known in European cultures. The former is perhaps more familiar, due in part to Peter Brook's 1985 stage play and subsequent 1989 film. The relative status of the two poems varies throughout India, with the *Ramayana* having a more widespread cultural currency in southeast Asia than the *Mahabharata*. They are similar to the poems of Homer in so far as they are written versions of a previous oral storytelling culture, but here the resemblance ends.

John Brockington describes how the two poems were retold in oral form over a long period of time (Brockington 1998: 3, 18–20). However, the written versions were also produced, rewritten and expanded over centuries. Brockington dates the events that are retold in both poems to around the eighth and ninth centuries BCE, with the earliest written versions being produced around the fourth century BCE. He also suggests that the *Ramayana* reached its final form before the *Mahabharata*, which was completed around the fourth century CE. The upshot is that both poems existed in bardic form for around 400 years, and then went through many revisions over several more centuries. In the case of the *Mahabharata*, the tale of those descended from the hero Bharata, this rewriting process may have taken another 800 years (Brockington 1998: 26–7). Brockington glosses his discussion as follows:

> In general terms, the didactic sections reveal an outlook close to that of classical Hinduism, in contrast to the older more sacrificial and *svarga*-oriented pattern of the older narrative passages.
>
> (Brockington 1998: 248)

He takes the multiple representations of religious ritual (the sacrifice) as a touchstone by which to differentiate the two levels of the text as we have it.

At the core of the *Mahabharata* is an epic story that probably originated in communal performances retelling the struggle for sovereignty between two sets of cousins. The senior line is comprised of the five virtuous orphaned Pandava brothers, known by this patronymic because of their father's name, Pandu. They lose their inheritance rights in a ritualised gambling match and are exiled for a period of 14 years (Smith 2009:121ff; see also

Brockington 1998: 187–8 for the ritualistic connotations of such a gambling match). Their cousins, the hundred Kauravas, are led by Duryodhana. They are the sons of Pandu's brother Dhritarashtra. Much of the first part of the narrative is concerned with the conflict between the Pandavas and their cousins even as they are all growing up. The second part (Smith 2009: 164ff) delineates the actions of the Pandava siblings in exile, particularly the three eldest: the Emperor Yudhishthira; the great archer Arjuna; and Bhima the strong. The other two (Nakula and Sahadeva) are twins, half-brothers to their elder siblings. After their time in the forest, which is a generic term meaning any uncivilised place of exile, they return to wage war on their cousins, whose defeat and deaths take up most of the rest of the story. There is a *coda* in the form of a postwar narrative section, which ends with everyone ascending to heaven. This overall narrative arc forms the bare bones of the text that has come down to us; a great deal more has been added. In structural terms, it could be characterised by comparison with the Homeric epics. The forest exile in the *Mahabharata* would be equivalent to the wanderings of Odysseus, and the war would be the equivalent of the *Iliad* (a point that is also made at Brockington 1998: 75–7). There is no siege of a great city, however, since the climactic battle takes place at an agreed location, the plain of Kurukshetra. Finally, the poem ends with a double homecoming as the winners return to power in their kingdom, and then achieve apotheosis. Smith's introduction to his edition of the poem gives a full narrative overview (Smith 2009: xv–xviii), and this can usefully be compared with Brockington's description (1998: 28–34).

However, there is a great deal more to the *Mahabharata* than this bare account would suggest. First, there are other major characters, many of whom are heroes of the first rank in their own right. Some of them fight for the Kauravas, even though they know that right (and ultimately, might) is on the side of the exiled Pandavas. Both sets of cousins grow up under the tutelage of Drona the teacher and he joins with Bhishma, who is uncle to both warring factions, being the brother of Pandu and Dhritarashtra. They represent the older generation of heroes, and both fight for the Kauravas even though they know they will lose. Another major hero who fights with them is Karna, who is half-brother to the Pandavas, although they do not know this until after his death. Many other characters make a serious impact on the combat at Kurukshetra, most of them sons of the other heroes. All of the heroes are represented as being able to wield celestial weapons, which are mostly manifestations of their mastery over themselves and their environment, and they usually achieve this mastery by means of ascetic practices. A few weapons of divine manufacture also exist, and are given to the appropriate heroes by the various gods.

The heroes who work with the Pandavas to recover their rightful inheritance include the greatest of all, Krishna, and his importance draws attention to the second crucial element: that of divinity. Unlike the Homeric epics, the main characters are not just children or descendants of the gods; they are avatars, or direct manifestations, although they are not necessarily always aware of this. The Kauravas are the enemies of the gods, demons reborn into human form after failing to defeat their celestial opponents. The Pandavas are incarnations of the rulers of the upper worlds, portions that the gods have bequeathed to humanity in order to defeat the demons. Yudhishthira, the leader of the Pandavas, is an avatar of the Lord of *Dharma*. Krishna is represented as the lord of all (Smith 2009: 106), and is paired with Arjuna. The two of them are also incarnations of the divine seers, Nara and Narayana. Confusingly, Arjuna is also the son of the god Indra. Krishna is reborn as a human many times in order to protect the world and its people from harm. He is completely invincible, but rather than fight directly, he acts as strategic adviser and as Arjuna's charioteer. For a full discussion of the complex identifications of the figure of Krishna and its context, see Smith (2009: xxxiv–xli) and also Brockington (1998: 262).

The third major component is the concept of *dharma*, a word that cannot be satisfactorily translated into English. In cosmological terms, it comprises the sum of all that is properly good in the world. During the course of the great cycle of ages, it decreases by natural rhythm across all four stages of the world's history. The world loses a quarter of its *dharma* per cycle until the

Age of Kali, the *kaliyuga*, which is inaugurated by the slaughter at Kurukshetra (Smith 2009: 17). There are similarities with classical Western conceptions of the golden, silver, bronze and iron ages such as those to be found in Hesiod. At the end of the fourth age, a cataclysm will renew creation and the endless cycle begins all over again. However, *dharma* is also an ethical category, delineating the behaviour that is appropriate to classes and individuals. The meaning here shades into the English term 'righteousness', although it should be borne in mind that the concept is relative to a person's position in society. In terms of the individual, *dharma* is attained as a form of relative freedom from the emotions. There are other concepts that are intrinsic to human life in the poem, but *dharma* is the most important. In comparative terms, it has equivalent importance to *kleos* in Greek epic, or *pietas* and *clementia* for the Romans. Its multiplicity in the *Mahabharata* is discussed in Brockington (1998: 242ff), who identifies a dynamic internal discussion of the concept:

> Indeed, it does seem to be the case that the epic is exploring the ability of the concept of *dharma* to provide a framework for social interaction and its adequacy to deal with varying situations.
>
> (Brockington 1998: 244)

The castes into which society is divided in the Sanskrit epics constitute the fourth main element of the *Mahabharata*. Most of the characters belong to the Kshatriya group, the warriors, kings, rulers and aristocracy. Generally speaking, it is their *dharma* to protect the people and their own rights, which means that they are expected to act as a warrior elite. They are also supposed to be special protectors of the second group, the Brahmins. The latter constitute an educated elite, although their education does not include the arts of warfare. The Sutra caste serves both of these two hierarchically superior social strata. Everyone else is placed in the fourth caste, which supports the others with its labour.

The fifth point is that the *Mahabharata* interweaves the caste system, the divine war, and *dharma*, into a dynamic and often contradictory exposition of the world it seeks to represent.

The reason for this is that all three of these have their own major ethical considerations, but if one predominates then it provides the ultimate foundation for the conflict in the celestial war between the gods and the demons (Smith 2009: 19–20). The concepts do not necessarily align gracefully. For example, it is possible for a given Sutra to be superior in *dharma* to a particular Brahmin, because the individual Sutra may fulfil his or her own *dharma* as a member of that caste, and the Brahmin may not be a true practitioner in his or her own situation. Such complexity inevitably results not only in the opposite condition, which is *adharma*, but also breaches of *dharma* by those who are supposed to uphold it. These moments are cruces in the story because human *dharma* is often overruled by the necessities of divine conflict, usually represented in the story as fate or destiny. Among other notable examples, it explains why Krishna advises Bhima to strike a low blow against Duryodhana when the two fight it out in single combat (Smith 2009: 549ff).

The reason for this complexity, and the contradictions that characterise it, are to be found in the centuries-long process of its textual evolution, as an early Kshatriya epic becomes overlaid and interspersed by the didactic concerns of the poem's Brahmin retractors (see Smith 2009: xiii). The result is an uneven (and incredibly long) poem that consists of two overlapping and sometimes oppositional narrative lines. In this process epic heroes who originally were probably so powerful that they were likened to the gods, in fact become avatars of specific gods. The pairing of Krishna and Arjuna is given precedence, and Krishna attains pre-eminence. This explains his central sermon, the group of chapters known as the *Bhagavadgita* (Smith 2009: 353ff; see also Brockington 1998: 267–77). The long death-bed sermon of Bhishma also belongs to this didactic layer (Smith 2009: 606ff). The result is a poem that combines both epic narration and moral/religious teaching. The *Mahabharata* conflates two traditions within itself, in a move that is radically different from the pairing of Homer and Hesiod in the Western tradition. In a long discursive section, John Brockington details the two main levels of the text as that of the earlier epic narrative, compounded with later didactic additions (Brockington 1998: 130ff).

His analysis continues with a useful historical overview of secondary treatments of the poem. He notes that the process is not smooth at all; indeed, the two layers are often in direct contradiction with one another, as evidenced in the multiple characterisations of Arjuna and Krishna (Brockington 1998: 159).

The final point that needs to be made concerns the role of women in the poem. Kunti, the mother of the Pandavas, gives birth to Karna as a result of being penetrated by the sun god. Her virginity is restored, but out of shame she abandons the baby. He is adopted and brought up by a Sutra family and becomes a kind of test case for cross-caste breeding and rivalry. It is only after his death that she admits to her other sons that he was in fact their half-brother. Draupadi (avatar of the goddess Shri) becomes wife to all five Pandavas one after another, with her virginity being miraculously restored after her first night with each husband because of her own fidelity to *dharma*. Women therefore function as another indication of the two layers of the poem, first because of their place as mothers and wives to aristocratic warrior kings, and second as avatars or ascetics in their own right. John Brockington sees the various characterisations of women as inflected by the two main textual levels, just as much as those of the men (Brockington 1998: 223–4).

In terms of literary technique, the *Mahabharata* makes use of the internal story as a significant form of exposition. This particular method is one way for the text to try to integrate its two layers. However, it is so common that it could be considered to be a cultural factor, perhaps descended from the earliest forms of the poem as delivered in communal recitations. When a character is asked to explain the reasoning behind a position, for example, they will then resort to telling a story as an oblique method to illustrate why they have decided to act as they do. The result is that the poem is peppered with short story interludes and digressions, a technique similar to that used by Ovid. However, it is so common that in many cases readers from other cultures can find it very difficult indeed to maintain the thread of the main storyline. This probably says more about the Western fetishising of assumed narrative coherence than it does about the *Mahabharata* itself, but it is still a factor in the reception of the text outside the Indian subcontinent. The logic of the internal story therefore goes much further than is the case with Ovid's use of it, so much so in fact that the poem has its own framing narrative, something it holds in common with the *Ramayana* (Smith 2009: xxiii). In fact, the story of Prince Rama appears as an interlude in the course of the *Mahabharata* (Smith 2009: 210–14) and Brockington characterises this all-pervasive mechanism with the use of the suggestive term "emboxing" (Brockington 1998: 18).

The framing narrative in the *Ramayana* is foregrounded. The bardic poet Valmiki claims the credit for this narrative procedure, and for versifying the poem as a whole, and assumptions about him and his status are very similar to those of Homer. It is tempting to perceive the *Ramayana* in a manner similar to the *Mahabharata*, as a set of verbal performances that are codified into a written form, which then itself undergoes a process of accretion. However, the very strong positioning of a narrator figure in the form of Valmiki challenges any such straightforward assumptions, as does the relative simplicity of the narrative itself. Internal stories are employed, but they do not appear with such frequency and consistency as they do in the *Mahabharata*. The basic text comprises the central five books of the *Ramayana*, with Valmiki's emboxing narrative describing Rama's childhood, and then finally bringing his story to an end with his ascension into heaven. He does seem to undergo similar cultural transformations to those of the characters in the *Mahabharata*, starting off as a great warrior leader, turning into a manifestation of Indra, and ultimately being subsumed as an avatar of Krishna. The process is equally uneven, and is interspersed across the poem as a whole, but unlike its partner epic, the *Ramayana* does not have quite the same propensity to didacticism, which may well be a result of this poem's attaining relatively fixed literary form at an earlier date.

The *Ramayana* has many of the same concerns as the *Mahabharata*, especially in relation to *dharma*. There are moments of narrative crisis at which Rama seems to act against *dharma*, emblematising it as a concept that is open to interpretation. Rama shoots the Monkey Lord Sugriva's brother Vali when the two brothers are in physical combat (Valmiki 2000: 329ff). As he lies dying, Vali castigates Rama for acting against the warrior's *dharma* by shooting him while he is distracted. Rama's response is that he had sworn to an alliance with Sugriva, and the *dharma* of alliance dictates that this has priority. This is important, because it puts in tension two major elements of what might constitute *dharma*, marking it as a relativistic concept. The episode also demonstrates that competing components of *dharma* can produce internal tension; in effect, Rama is presented with an ethical choice and either possibility would lay him open to criticism. Furthermore, there is an earlier textual hint that human *dharma* may not in any case be entirely applicable to the world outside civilisation: "We must learn to respect the code of behaviour of the world we now inhabit," as Sita says to Rama and Lakshmana after they have entered the forest (Valmiki 2000: 234). Such relativism prepares the way for ensuing conflict, which is very reminiscent of the moment of crisis for tragic heroes in Greek drama. For example, in the *Oresteia*, Orestes is obliged by divine law to avenge his father Agamemnon's murder and at the same time is equally required not to kill his mother Clytemnestra, the murderer. However, the Sanskrit epics incorporate this sort of dilemma in a way that differs from Western literary treatments, by means of the concept of *dharma*. A useful statement of these issues occurs when Rama takes up residence as an ascetic in the forest: "A king must do what will benefit his subjects, even if it is unrighteous, for such is his duty" (Valmiki 2000: 46). Brockington sees the conception of *dharma* changing from a secular to a religious one:

> Probably its earlier meaning can best be paraphrased as 'a pillar of the establishment', in which the emphasis is on *dharma* as the proper social order and even political stability, whereas later the aspect of *dharma* as moral values, almost to the exclusion of other sides of its meaning, leads to its being interpreted as denoting 'righteous Rama', the ethical paragon.
>
> (Brockington 1998: 464–5)

The discussion here is very much in keeping with the multiple layers produced by the uneven centuries-long rewriting process that is enacted upon both epics. This would explain why Rama tests Sita by fire after she is rescued, checking that she has behaved with propriety during her captivity. Later on, in the framing narrative, his *dharma* as a husband is in conflict with his *dharma* as a ruler, since now the people are murmuring against her. As a result, he banishes her. She returns at the end of the poem and is taken into the earth, just as the two bards who are telling Valmiki's tale turn out to be twin sons Sita bore for Rama after being expelled. Rama is then assumed into heaven. The complexity presented here has a great deal to do with the poem's narrative levels, especially later written additions to the epic text.

As well as adding a framing narrative, a similar Brahminical operation is enacted to that which takes place in the *Mahabharata*. Elements of this layer are interspersed throughout the text, and can be characterised in terms of yet another divine war. Vishnu is approached by the rest of the gods to find a way of dealing with the invulnerable Rakshasa Ravana, and takes human form specifically in order to slay Ravana. Rama and his brothers are all portions of this supreme deity, while at the same time another textual layer links Rama with Indra and even Shiva. Rama is therefore made into another incarnation of the same divinity as Krishna in the *Mahabharata*, and in this reading, Sita is an incarnation of Vishnu's consort Lakshmi. The shape-changing monkeys are incarnations of lesser divinities, born to aid Vishnu in his task (Valmiki 2000: 31). The monkey hero Hanuman is the son of the Wind, and again terms of fate and destiny intertwine with this supernatural dimension in the war against Ravana. A symptom of these layers is the use of multiple internal stories. Even so, the relatively straightforward heroic narrative of the *Ramayana* combines with its less complex textual history to produce a more straightforward overall epic treatment. The two poems have some overlapping concerns, but they are not identical.

In her translator's note to the *Ramayana*, Arshia Sattar describes a temptation for translations to use archaisms. She writes:

> We must try and remember as we translate epics and traditional story literatures that even at their times of composition, these were

> not obscure texts meant for scholarly elites. They were living, vibrant
> and were composed in a language accessible to all kinds of people.
>
> (Sattar 2000a: x)

Of course, she has in mind the Indian epics as opposed to the literary conventions familiar from Latin, although her comments are also appropriate to the Homeric tradition. However, the subsequent production of literary versions of communal verbal artefacts does not necessarily lead to textual ossification. This at least is demonstrated by what we know of the Mesopotamian epics. In other cases, of course, it can have this effect. In any event, the differentiation between cultural epic productions must be maintained, since the field of epic is vast and generalisations have to be resisted if cultural specificity is to be respected. This is not easy to do and a dynamic conception of epic is needed in order to cope with its multivalent variations. This is why epic cannot be defined in narrowly formalist terms, but it also explains why non-poetic texts (e.g. the Bible) can fulfil the function of epic for their given culture. When subsequent cultures reinterpret an epic text for their own consumption, they produce and re-produce the logic of translation to which Sattar refers. The meanings associated with an epic can become layered as a consequence of later accretions and the cultural assumptions that produce them; in the case of the Sanskrit epics, there is the added difficulty posed by multiple rewritings. The meanings that are generated by such processes lay the epic open to different kinds of appropriation. In this context, it is perhaps more fruitful to see the epic function as a kind of negotiated space, criss-crossed and contested by different interests. On the one hand there is the axis of communality-literacy; on the other, there is the axis of formal requirements such as the shift from poetry to prose. In the ancient period the poetic form predominates, but that does not preclude the possible development of prose epics. It is perhaps most useful to comprehend the epic as produced in the cultural space between these two types of continuum. Together, they constitute the conditions of possibility for the epic function.

3

FROM THE HEROIC TOWARDS
ROMANCE AND ALLEGORY

Epic forms develop and change throughout the period often
designated as 'the Middle Ages'. However, this historical term is
of limited use when applied to the wide variations that exist
across the continuum from oral to literary epic. The reason for
this is that the medieval period only makes sense in Western
European conceptions of a long epoch between the fall of the
Roman Empire and the emergence of the Renaissance. Even so,
the situation is further compounded when deciding what defines
either end of the period. Rome fell several times; the Eastern
Roman Empire lasted until 1453; and the Renaissance gathered
momentum in different countries at different times. The various
epics that were produced during this time need to be treated in
relation to their specific historical contexts. This is especially true
for those texts that do not belong to the post-Roman world, since
they are not influenced by the classical tradition so familiar from
Homer and Virgil. Epic narratives that come from Norse and
Celtic cultures are obvious examples, especially because of their
roots in oral composition, but they are not the only alternatives.

The Persian *Shah-Namah* is especially important in this regard, since it represents a highly sophisticated literary culture with its own epic narratives. The *Shah-Namah* embodies a particularly Persian sensibility, incorporating into its themes the rise of Islam.

THE *SHAH-NAMAH*

We have seen in Chapter 2 that elements that will become common in epic poetry can already be discerned in very early examples such as *Gilgamesh*. Epics from various cultures share aspects in common, *motifs* such as the journey, combat and the role of women. Formal, structural elements evolve and develop as the Latin poets build upon the Greek inheritance, especially the beginning of the narrative *in medias res* and the formal invocation to the muse as source of inspiration. The French structuralist critic and theorist Gerard Genette takes issue with the Aristotelian downgrading of epic when compared with tragedy in his book *The Architext* (first published in France in 1979). Genette argues that Aristotle reacted against Plato's undeveloped distinction between genres by constructing a hier-archy that privileges tragedy over what he calls the "mixed genre" of epic (Genette 1992: 9). For Genette, the two are different treatments of the same subject matter: "The superior-dramatic defines tragedy, the superior-narrative defines epic" (13), with "superior" here being understood as the representation of socially important characters. Genette goes on to explore the relationship between tragedy and epic by concentrating on their narrative functions (21ff). Although he is at pains to rework classical genre theory, Genette constructs a framework that allows for typological comparison between epic works from different cultures.

Bearing Genette's framework in mind, it is possible to compare an epic such as the *Shah-Namah* with the classical Western tra-dition. There is still no fully satisfactory English translation of the whole of Fardusi's Iranian epic poem, although several abridged editions do exist. One easily available text is by Alexander Rogers that was originally published in 1907, but has more recently been reissued (Fardusi 1995). It takes the form of translated poetic sections interspersed with prose summaries, and as Rogers notes in his introduction, the poem was written in the decades around the beginning of the tenth century CE, with most of the earlier periods adapted from a pre-existing poem by Fardusi's predecessor Dakiki (Rogers in Fardusi 1995: xi). It covers the history of the Persian kings right up to the time of the Islamic conquest, ending with the reign of Yazdagird III (died c.652 CE, murdered by his own troops).

The *Shah-Namah* begins with a prayer to Allah, which in terms of its formal placement is equivalent to an invocation to the muse. Next comes a creation myth, followed by a broadly mythological initial section in which the earliest Persian kings invent iron-working, irrigation, spinning, animal husbandry, writing, warfare and the mud brick. All of these events take place within the overall context of a war against Ahriman, a principle of darkness and evil who is similar to the figure of Satan in Christianity. He is supported by the Divs, a servitor race that functions as demons. As the poem progresses, the Divs come to resemble a rival civilisation and they are often pressed into service by the early hero-kings, usually as the result of conquest.

The remainder of the *Shah-Namah* is divided into two main parts. The first consists of a narrative of legendary heroes and kings, the greatest of whom is Rustam. He himself belongs to a major family and is treated as a king in his own right, although he supports the central Kai kings, the Achaemenid dynasty that founded the Iranian Empire. They are familiar from the writings of their Greek enemies, and are implicitly accorded superiority over all other kings. The relationship between Rustam and the Kai kings bears comparison with similar narrative structures in the epic poems of other cultures such as the *Iliad*, in which the main war leader of the invading Greeks, Agamemnon, is supported by a major hero figure (Achilles), without whom eventual success would be impossible.

The terms 'Iranian' and 'Persian' both refer interchangeably to the culture of the empire produced by the merging of the Medes and Persians in the sixth century BCE, which also appears in the Old Testament in the story of the destruction of Babylon. The narrative of Rustam's family takes up a major portion of this part of the poem, from his grandfather Sam right through to Rustam's death (Fardusi 1995: 66ff), and the narratives here resemble those of Herakles in the Greek tradition, especially with regard to some of the details of the wooing of Rubadah, daughter of the King of Kabul, by Sam's son Zal. The importance accorded this marriage can be compared with the events immediately prior to the birth of Herakles, who will have to perform his famous labours on behalf of an inferior man, King Eurystheus, another instance of the *motif* of the powerful hero and weaker, but socially superior, king. The adult Rustam undertakes a journey that turns into a series of seven challenges that include an archetypal dragon-killing and an encounter with a sorceress who lives in an enchanted garden (Fardusi 1995: 132–62). Later, Rustam fathers a son, Suhrab, who grows up in the land of the Turks. When they invade Iran, Suhrab leads their army as the main hero and is eventually and unwittingly killed by his own father (167–99). This is a particularly important moment in the poem as a whole, because it condenses what has become a fairly consistent theme in this epic, that of familial (and thus dynastic) conflict. In this respect the *Shah-Namah* shares some of the concerns of the Greek legend of Oedipus.

Structural elements such as the journey, the trials of the hero and the hero's subordination to a less heroic king continue in the *Shah-Namah* with a repetition of Rustam's feats in the form of the seven trials of Prince Asfandyar, heir to the throne (308–41), who is promised the kingdom by his father the Kai if he succeeds. However, when the prince returns in triumph, his father orders him to attack Rustam, because he wishes to retain the crown for himself. The fact that this epic pattern of a weaker king fearful of the superior prowess of a greater hero surfaces repeatedly marks the *Shah-Namah* as inheriting a formal narrative technique from an age-old storytelling tradition, which demonstrates how migrating narratives recur in widely disparate epic traditions. Rustam does try to avert the conflict but Asfandyar obeys his father, even though he knows it will lead to his own death. Olga M. Davidson compares this treatment of the conflict between the hero Rustam and the Persian kings with that between Achilles and Agamemnon as a common epic *motif* (Davidson 2009).

After Rustam's death, and before the narrative moves on to the much later Sasanian dynasty, Alexander of Macedon (Sekander in the poem) appears in a sort of interlude. Fardusi's seemingly haphazard chronicling of the relationship between Iran and the West can seem very puzzling to readers steeped in the traditions of Eurocentric historiography, especially given the importance accorded Alexander as conqueror of the entire Persian Empire. Even though most of the text up to this point details the activities of the Kai kings, very few of them are recognisable as the more familiar dynastic line of Persian kings who encountered the Greeks. Indeed, the first to be connected and more easily recognised in this way is the king who is destroyed by Sekander, Dara (known as Darius to the Greeks). The Sekander episode epitomises the poem's conceptual relationship with the west. Philip II (Alexander's father) is known as Filkus in the *Shah-Namah*; he is described as "king of Rum, an ally of the king of Rus" (Fardusi 1995: 352) who attacks Amuriyah, a town that was possibly situated in what is now modern Iraq, and belonging in the narrative to the Persian kings. Filkus makes peace with King Darab of Persia, who gives the interloper the hand of his daughter Nahid in marriage (353); from this union is born Sekander. He will go on to conquer the Persian kingdom of King Dara, son of Darab, Sekander's cousin. The *Shah-Namah* reworks this historical material in the form of an epic narrative, from the perspective of Persian tradition. This explains the episodic nature of the poem's epic narrative of these half-remembered historical events and personages, who are recast into the familiar forms of epic heroes and kings.

Philip II, however, was not king of Rum, because Rum (the Roman Empire) as such did not yet exist, and neither did the kingdom of the Rus. "Filkus" did not invade Persia, and he certainly never married a Persian princess. However, these issues must be related to the literary and cultural norms of Fardusi's Persia around the tenth century CE. The Persian Empire prior to the appearance of Alexander controlled some of the longest civilised areas in the world at the time, including Mesopotamia and Egypt, in addition to the Greek Ionian cities of Asia Minor. Compared with this history, anything to the west of this empire would be, to a Persian, little more than a hazy collection of half-memories. This explains the extreme anachronisms that pepper the poem as a whole, and not just the Sekander section. In the mythic part of the poem, Arab horses appear very early on (Fardusi 1995: 22), and the Alan tribal group is mentioned (63). In the section that follows, Greek brocade is mentioned (74) during the wooing of Rubadah by Zal. War elephants are extremely common, (121 ff.), and the Turks and Turkomans appear throughout the poem, up to and including the more historical period of the Sasanians (127, 295 and 438). The Khakan is mentioned several times as leader of these peoples from central Asia (for example at 221 and 516), and is often confused with armies from China. The stirrup is mentioned during the career of Rustam (235), an element of horse furniture that is thought to have been invented during the era of migrations following the emergence of the Huns, many hundreds of years after the time of Rustam. References to the Kaiser appear very frequently (280, 305, 398, 400–1, 415, 479, 505 and 511) and earlier inclusions of this particular detail are clearly anachronistic, as are the references to Constantinople that accompany some of them. These are not simply minor historical details, since each of them represents an important moment in Persian, and indeed world history, but the poem conflates them in ways that defy recognisable historical linearity.

Clearly, Fardusi is reinterpreting previous epochs in Persian history in the terms familiar to his contemporaries, hence the reference to the Rus and, especially, Rum and the Kaiser. His conception of Roman territory is nebulous at best, as is the title of its ruler, which is clearly Rogers' rendering of the Iranian transliteration of the name of Caesar. So too is the time period within which the Roman Empire to the west exists in the poem. Similar narrative inconsistencies underpin the representation of the other main external threat to Persia, that from the central Asian steppes. Territories that are peripheral to Persia throughout its history, as well as specific details, are thus redefined and assimilated in a manner appropriate to Fardusi's own time. The *Shah-Namah* provides a narrative appropriate to the local historical context of the poet in a recognisably epic format, a synthesis of various elements into a form capable of incorporating migrating narratives and epic *motifs* into itself.

The geographical and historical centrality of Persia is therefore a 'given' in the poem, and the main interest is in internal affairs with even the intrusion of the Macedonians being given a Persian gloss. By making Sekander the son of a Persian princess, Fardusi (or more likely his predecessor Dakiki) explains away the external invasion and the sudden collapse of Dara's kingdom. The whole episode becomes one more in a succession of internal conflicts, and thus is unified thematically by a prominent strand that runs right through the representation of Persian history. The poem reduces the importance of foreign intervention, by glossing over the minor role played by Persia proper as a province of Alexander's Seleucid successors, as well as the accession of the Parthian Arsacid dynasty. As an epic narrative of Persian history, the *Shah-Namah* needs to demonstrate the superior longevity of the Persian state, and so the poem functions as a foundation narrative for Persia similar to what the *Aeneid* does for Rome. For example, Rogers notes in one of his prose passages the way in which the Seleucids are relegated to only a brief mention:

> There is now related the history of the dynasty of the Ashkaris, which endured some 200 years. They go by the name of the Murklu Tartaif, or Miscellaneous Kings, from not being all of the same race.
>
> (Fardusi 1995: 390)

The overall impression is therefore one of relatively smooth continuity from the Kai kings, through Sekander, on into the Sasanians; at which point the capital of this final dynasty, Ctesiphon, is first mentioned (399), and the city is referred to frequently thereafter. The epic privileges Iranian ruling dynasties by treating centuries of foreign domination almost as an irrelevance in the grand scheme of things, and in this respect the *Shah-Namah* engages in a national narrative that bears comparison with the *Aeneid*, both in national and dynastic terms.

Like the later Achaemenids and the Arsacids before them, the Sasanians were Zoroastrians, a monotheistic religion in which evil is represented by the figure of Ahriman who is prominent early on in the *Shah-Namah*. This religion is dealt with in some detail (283ff), especially when it supersedes the older religion of fire worship, albeit after a struggle. However, as with geography and history, the poem registers other religions in a haphazard way, and again for the same reason, that they are not central to the Persian experience. Angels are mentioned as messengers from the divine (8, 47 and 273); judgement day and the final resurrection appear (121), and there are explicit references to Moses, first as a prophet (127), and again when the baby Darab is set adrift in a basket on the Euphrates (351). Christian elements appear with increasing frequency from this point onwards (400ff) as they figure more and more prominently in opposition to the later Persian rulers. The *Shah-Namah* incorporates elements of different cultures into its epic narrative as a way of addressing issues of concern to its own location.

A sophisticated understanding of external threats to Persia under the Sasanians emerges in the final section of the poem. One reason for this is that the historical details are closer to the time of writing. Additionally, military practice in times of war provides a context for heroism, a central feature in the composition of the epic hero. The encroachment of the Kaiser from the west coincides with a resumption of warfare in central Asia with the so-called Turks. They are probably a conflation of the Hephthalite Huns with the first historical appearances of the Turks themselves, whose name Fardusi uses because they are his own very familiar contemporaries. The simultaneous attacks lead to war on two fronts (especially at 453 and 487), and the seriousness of this situation is compounded by internal struggles between the Sasanians and pretenders to the throne, as represented in the figure of Behram, who manages to be declared king by acclamation of swords (507). In the midst of this ongoing crisis comes a prophecy of the coming of the prophet Mohammed (482), followed by the inexorable rise of Islam (542ff). The culmination of Persian history in the Islamic world marks the *Shah-Namah* as an epic myth of origins. In structural terms, Islam functions in the same way as the emergence of Augustus in the *Aeneid*. The Persian poem does not utilise the sophisticated time-scheme of Virgil's poem in order to accomplish this end. Instead, the dissolution of the Sasanian state marks the beginning of a new era in much the same way as the death of Turnus and the marriage of Aeneas and Lavinia.

HEROIC EPIC AND SAGA

The case of the *Shah-Namah* shows that epic continued to evolve outside the Western tradition, while the sagas demonstrate that this tradition was not monolithic. As a category, the saga is possibly even more difficult to delineate than epic. For example, the term 'saga' has become overloaded with subsequent associations in ways that are analogous to epic, particularly in the era of television (see Chapter 5). As oral stories that are subsequently written down, the sagas could be said to constitute a subset of epic more generally, although their formal properties differ, especially since they are in prose. 'Oral' here means not only communal, but familial, since many of the sagas were produced by families settling Iceland. In this way they can be related in historical and cultural terms to what has often been termed the European periphery of the Germanic and Norse-Icelandic peoples. By analogy, they have features in common with Irish and Welsh Celtic Christian texts based on pre-Christian tales. A saga is usually the story of a single hero's personal adventures within an overall context of low level warfare such as raiding and feuds. Outright national or tribal wars do occur, or are mentioned, but they are not necessarily the main focus of the narrative. It is true that the sagas contain just as many Christian elements as the epics and romances that are produced in other parts of Europe and in some of the same areas later on. However, what sets them apart from their Latinate cousins is the way in which they relate to Christianity.

There are two elements to such a conception of the saga: the first is the individual story's roots in a recognisably pagan past, and the second is how that past is incorporated at the moment of its transcription in literary form within a Christian cultural context. The coincidence of the two can be relatively harmonious, or it can produce a sense of conflict, in which some pagan elements can seem at odds with the Christian surface. For example, although *Beowulf* was written by and for the Christian *milieu* of later Anglo-Saxon England, the pagan Scandinavian past that is represented in the poem differs from the ways in which the *Song of Roland* harks back to the period in which that epic is set, as opposed to the one for which it was written. This can partly be explained by the location of the French poem within a Romanised epic tradition that is not available to the Old English poet of *Beowulf*; hence the term 'romance' and its descendant, the 'roman', which even now remains a French synonym for the novel. Also, and this is no minor point, the France that produced the text of the *Song of Roland* had been Christian for a great deal longer than the England of the Anglo-Saxon *Beowulf*. The *Song of Roland* is a later Christian literary representation of an already Christian past, while *Beowulf* reworks elements of the pagan past, especially codes of political and moral leadership.

It is precisely this relationship between pagan antecedents and the Christian present of the written text that underpins *Beowulf* as a whole. This poem is not a Norse-Icelandic saga, but it can usefully be compared with its linguistic cousins. *Beowulf* is broadly composed of three main parts involving the hero's three combats, first with Grendel, then with Grendel's mother (who remains unnamed), and finally with the dragon. In his 1967 essay "The Interlace Structure of *Beowulf*", John Leyerle investigates the poem's structure in detail (Leyerle 2002), and he takes as his starting point the interlaced pattern so common in Anglo-Saxon jewellery and weapons, suggesting that *Beowulf* is analogous to Anglo-Saxon ornamental style. According to Jane Chance, in another essay included in the same volume, the poem's structure is centrally modulated by means of feminine figures of the hearth and hall, who counterpoint the aggressively masculine activities of the hero (Chance 2002), much as Christianity can be seen to domesticate the pagan heroic *ethos*. The world inhabited by these personages is clearly denoted as belonging to a relatively valorised and coherently represented pagan past. As Seamus Heaney notes in his Translator's Introduction to *Beowulf*, "The poem was written in England but the events it describes are set in Scandinavia, in a 'once upon a time' that is partly historical" (Heaney 2002: xxii), but it is saturated with Christian imagery and terminology, all of which is derived from the Old Testament (Heaney 2002: xxx). This is especially true, as Heaney realises, for the *Beowulf* poet's reimagining of the pagan past, as he makes use of pre-Christian Judaic antiquity as a touchstone for a story from a previous epoch.

The hero Beowulf might be a pagan, but he is still a good man in terms that would be instantly recognisable to the poem's contemporary audience. Fred C. Robinson suggests that the double funeral of Beowulf will remind those audiences of pagan heroic apotheosis (Robinson 2002), the moment at which the hero's almost divine status is assured. Even so, the poem does comment fairly negatively at times upon pagan practice:

> That was their way,
> Their heathenish hope; deep in their hearts
> They remembered hell. The Almighty Judge
> Of good deeds and bad, the Lord God,
> Head of the Heavens and High King of the World,
> Was unknown to them.

> (Donoghue 2002: 7).

Here the poetic persona intrudes on the narrative to ensure that even these pagans can have some intimation of good and evil. The conflation of pagan and Christian aspects cannot be lightly dismissed as contradictions in the text, since they constitute a structuring element. In his essay on this topic, Thomas D. Hill thinks that the poem is relatively relaxed when it comes to the relationship between Christianity and paganism (Hill 2002: 201–2), while Roberta Frank argues for an internal logic of structuration that is produced via the tension between pagan and Christian elements (Frank 2002). In fact, she even goes so far as to suggest that the mixed representation of religious *mores* in the poem's version of Scandinavia is analogous to the state of Anglo-Saxon England at the time of the poem's writing, especially the political structure of the emerging English nation-state, where multiple clan and tribal groups are shown to be in constant rivalry, vying with one another for supremacy in an ongoing balance of alliances and warfare. Frank sees *Beowulf* as a communal narrative, a kind of national epic rooted in a semi-realised past that is not imperial. This is a different situation from the emphasis in the Virgilian epic on empire, because in the later text there is no overarching imperial superpower.

Similar points to those Frank makes about the pagan/Christian dichotomy in *Beowulf* have also been made about another Anglo-Saxon poem, *The Battle of Maldon*, especially in terms of its roots in a pagan warrior *ethos*. After the death of the war leader Byrhtnoth, his elite bodyguards continue the battle, which is suggested by one editor to be an act of revenge for his death (Griffiths 2000: 6). Griffiths further notes the importance of recovering the dead lord's body for a proper Christian burial, and the struggle over the corpse is a momentary elision of the ethics of two worlds, the pagan and the Christian, which is reminiscent of the burial of Beowulf. The comparison with *Beowulf* is especially enlightening, since the Scandinavian hero is mortally wounded by the dragon precisely because all but one of his bodyguards flee. Given the imprecision regarding dates for *The Battle of Maldon*, Griffiths speculates that an early date for its composition could imply that it is intended "to inspire resistance to the Vikings" (Griffiths 2000: 6). It is important to realise that both poems belong to a cultural tradition that is not defined in relation to Roman antiquity, as Griffiths notes of *The Battle of Maldon*:

> *Maldon* is one of a small group of 'battle' poems in Old English, Welsh and Old Norse, whose interrelationship is uncertain. It is not a genre obviously pioneered in Latin literature, and this may help account for the simplicity or directness of the diction, verse-patterns and sentence structure in the poem.
>
> (Griffiths 2000: 10)

As with the *Shah-Namah*, these texts provide alternatives to the Latin epic tradition and they continue to exist during the medieval period.

There are also parallels between *The Battle of Maldon* and the Old Welsh epic poem, *The Gododdin* (Aneirin 1994). Both poems tell the story of a lost battle and both have elements of the heroic warrior ethos associated with pre-Christian cultures. Furthermore, *The Gododdin* manuscript dates from the thirteenth century, and thus is even later than either *The Battle of Maldon* or *Beowulf*, although here the similarities end. *The Gododdin* is very much the product of a pagan Celtic (Brythonic) oral culture, and the narrative persona is the only survivor of the defeat. Unlike the Anglo-Saxon battle poem, the Welsh poet celebrates a resolutely non-Christian world of heroic combat, in which the ultimate accolade is to die in battle. In his translation of the poem, Steve Short notes the way in which the poem fuses the epic tradition with a direct narrative voice:

> The Gododdin is written within a traditional framework, and makes use of repeated epithets of the kind we find in, say, The Iliad. But the Gododdin is peculiar in comparison with other epic poetry on two counts: firstly, because it celebrates a defeat, not a victory; secondly, because of its deeply personal, elegiac tone.
>
> (Short in Aneirin 1994: 8)

The poem therefore has elements in common with other epics written down after a long life as part of an oral tradition.

A similar approach should be adopted with the Norse-Icelandic sagas, since as a form of heroic literature, they do conform to the familiar pattern of oral stories that are written down at a later date. Jon Karl Helgason reminds us that the sagas performed a communal function:

> In these few lines, Laxness gives a good idea of the roles the sagas may have played in the lives of the common people in Iceland in earlier times. First of all, they supplied them with suitable role models; second, they provided them with a nobler ancestry; and third, they offered a Golden Age of the past as a counter to contemporary miseries.
>
> (Helgason 2007: 65)

Here he is drawing attention to comments made by the critic Halldór Laxness. Similarly, Robert Cook notes in his Introduction to *Njal's Saga*:

As with the Homeric epics and the *Song of Roland*, well-remembered historical events were passed down through several centuries of oral tradition and finally shaped by the hand of a master story-teller and writer into a *non*-historical work of art.

(Cook 2001: ix)

This harking back to a previous age that is superior to the present operates as a kind of myth of origins. The sagas manage the relationship between the semi-mythic past and the all too real present. Vesteinn Olason describes how these stories about well-known families work to accommodate the past to the present, and indeed many of them have become known in English as 'family sagas' (Olason 2007). The term 'saga' itself is related to the English word to 'say', and it is important to realise that it encompasses the techniques of saying or telling a story. The narrative requirements of saga are historically and culturally specific, but they are also more diverse as a body than might at first appear to be the case. Torfi H. Tulinius presents a lucid overview of sagas that deal with the establishment of the Icelandic community and the country's Norse antecedents. He discusses manuscript culture and carefully notes the various stages in the production of what has come down to us as a seemingly homogeneous narrative tradition (Tulinius 2007: 449–52).

In the history of epic the sagas are important because they occupy a transitional position between oral communal narratives and their audiences on the one hand, and an emerging literary culture on the other. However, the sagas cannot be reduced to a straightforward relationship between the literary present and the communal oral past. Many of them are about very specific families and the historical or pseudo-historical events that befall them, but even those sagas that appear to deploy a form of literary realism contain elements of the supernatural. Some deal explicitly with legendary personages and times, but the one feature that marks the sagas as distinctive is the fact that they are written in prose, although many of them do contain poetic elements. This further differentiates them from the poetic works of the classical Western European epic tradition. In his Introduction to the Penguin

Classics edition of the sagas Robert Kellogg notes the conjunction of epic and saga when he argues that:

> Epic and saga are enough alike to make a comparison interesting and instructive, especially in the degree to which both genres synthesize history, myth, ethical values, and descriptions of actual life. Sagas differ from romance, the other great medieval narrative mode, by focusing attention on actual social types of people in a historically and geographically precise context, with little apparent interest in fantasy and the spiritual and psychological experience of what is sometimes called 'courtly love'.
>
> (Kellogg 2001: xviii)

The contiguity between epic and saga differentiates the latter (and by implication epic as well) from romance, especially in terms of the emphasis that is placed by Kellogg on courtly love as the defining feature of romance. In effect, he uses a comparative methodology to note that all three forms fulfil important and differing functions during this period. Indeed, in this respect, and recalling David Quint's observations on epic and empire discussed earlier in Chapter 2, it is possible to note these forms and their functions with some historical and cultural precision.

There are several stylistic elements common to the various sagas. One is the relative absence of a narrative voice; Kellogg notes that "The anonymity of their authors has become a feature of their style" (Kellogg 2001: xxv). He continues:

> There is rarely a disjunction in the art of the *Islendinga sogur* between our sense of the events they describe and the method of their telling, as if their language were a clear window on to the world of the saga.
>
> (Kellogg 2001: xxv)

However, Kellogg goes on to show that the relative sparseness of the style in the saga as a genre masks great subtlety of exposition, structure and characterisation. The story is usually one of "[...] a conflict that arises out of what are usually the events of everyday life in Iceland" (Kellogg 2001: xxxviii). The twin motors are personal honour and the family feud: "Honour (*saemd*) is to the conception of character in the sagas as feud is to the plot" (Kellogg 2001: xxxix), and the idea of honour is relatively elastic, encompassing general reputation, among other things (Kellogg 2001: xxxix–xlii). This gives great scope for multiple conflicts, especially when honour intersects with the exigencies of the family feud.

In common with epic traditions from other cultures, there is often an underlying element of the supernatural, even in the family sagas. Njal the Burnt, the titular main character of *Njal's Saga*, is a speaker of truths that are both actual and prophetic. In fact, Robert Cook argues that the *motif* of truth-saying is fundamental to this saga in that it seems to be particularly preoccupied with problems of the veracity or otherwise of representation (see Cook 2001: xvi–xix). *Njal's Saga* is also concerned with the pivotal role played by women and the two *motifs* come together in a complex web of jealousy, honour, masculinity, femininity, slander and truth (Cook 2001: xx), all of which issues are condensed into a central concern with the law and its inability to manage simmering social tensions. According to Cook, "Old hostilities, lying under the surface but waiting to erupt in bloodshed, constitute the underlying narrative thread" (Cook 2001: xxv). The relationship between these hostilities and the law is crucial to the double structure of *Njal's Saga*: "The two greatest crises in the saga, the death of Gunnar and the burning at Bergthorshvol, both occur when an arbitrated agreement has been broken" (Cook 2001: xxvi–xxvii). The sagas bear comparison with the deep-seated familial and dynastic tensions of Greek tragedy, for example in that between Thyestes and Atreus.

Of course, not all of the sagas are set only in Iceland. For example, *Egil's Saga* has ostensible similarities with *Njal's Saga* in terms of its emphasis on the importance of the family, but it also incorporates a great deal of travel. This is appropriate, because unlike Njal, Egil is a warrior as well as a poet, and he also represents an important stage in the development of Icelandic society according to Svanhildur Oskarsdottir:

> Although the saga brings together many different issues, its over-
> arching theme is the struggle of independent farmers against
> overbearing kings.
>
> (Oskarsdottir 2004: viii)

The foundation myth of Iceland involves the flight to freedom of various leaders and nobles from the iron rule of Harald Fairhair, King of Norway. It is crucial to note that the commonwealth that was subsequently consolidated is in the process of breaking down at the time of the writing of the sagas.

In her introduction to Bernard Scudder's translation of the text, Oskarsdottir describes how the story of Egil's family fits into a pattern of resistance and then emigration (Oskarsdottir 2004: ix–x), and this becomes the context for the figure of Egil himself, making him into a kind of test case as a founding father. Events that occur in the earlier history of the family are repeated during Egil's own lifetime, so much so that, as Oskarsdottir notes, such repetition works as a kind of unifying principle (xiii–xiv). *Egil's Saga* therefore has a bipartite structure, which is strikingly similar to the stories of Gunnar and Njal in *Njal's Saga*.

Another feature shared by the two texts is their emphasis on the function of women who, although excluded from power, have a crucial symbolic role, due to their position as objects of exchange in a masculine world (Oskarsdottir 2004: xxvii). Patriarchy of course relies on the subject position ascribed to women to remain stable, but even when women are supposedly deprived of social power, they remain the focus of masculine anxiety, which is especially true of Queen Gunnhild, who is the real obstacle that Egil must overcome. She is at least as intelligent and single-minded as Egil, and the conflict between them takes up a large part of the action. In this respect, *Egil's Saga* replicates a familiar epic concern with the politics of femininity.

The sagas share with the epic a deep concern with lineage, which underpins the importance of both family and feud in *Njal's Saga* and which expands into the sphere of political resistance in *Egil's Saga*. Lineage and politics are of fundamental concern to the *Orkneyinga Saga*, which is a kind of political family history of the Earls of Orkney (Palsson and Edwards 1981). The *Orkneyinga Saga* becomes more and more historically reliable the closer it gets to the time of writing. In the later parts of the narrative events are driven by inheritance, power and kinship relations, as Hermann Palsson and Paul Edwards observe:

> The recurrent theme, linked as we have said to the opening sections on the legendary Nor and Gor and their sons, is the division of the earldom between two, sometimes three ambitious men, and the breaking up and re-assembling of power groups.
>
> (Palsson and Edwards 1981: 15)

The various political manoeuvres that these tensions generate often bring the earldom into contact and conflict with other powers, especially Norway. This is the same context that is at work in *Egil's Saga*, but at a much higher social level.

The relatively exalted position occupied by the earls and their extended families also places them in a wider European cultural and political framework than is the case in most other sagas. It produces an interesting literary moment when Earl Rognvald goes on a crusade. Here, as Palsson and Edwards note, the saga form intersects with the romance, but it does so in a very specific way. En route to the Holy Land, Earl Rognvald is served at a feast in Narbonne by the unmarried Queen Ermingerd. He sits her on his knee and recites an impromptu verse to her:

> I'll swear, clever sweetheart,
> you're a slender delight
> to grasp and to cuddle,
> my golden-locked girl.
> Ravenous the hawk, crimson-
> claw'd, flesh-cramm'd –
> but now, heavily hangs
> the silken hair.
>
> (Palsson and Edwards 1981: 166)

The reference to the bloody hawk might seem unusual in a romance, but we should bear in mind that this Earl and his crewmembers are as much Vikings as pilgrims or crusaders.

In the words of the editors: "[...] it doesn't take long for Rognvald to get his hands on her and his praises are hardly those of a courtly gentleman" (Palsson and Edwards 1981: 17). The behaviour of Rognvald and his men suggests that the old pagan habits are still strong, even for men who are supposedly going on crusade; despite the romance elements, Rognvald's manners are anything but courtly. It is the juxtaposition of the two forms that provides much of the humour.

The saga that is most concerned with the pagan past is *The Saga of the Volsungs* (Byock 1990). Unlike the family sagas that are set in the period of the colonisation of Iceland, this is one has its roots much further back, during the Germanic migrations at the end of antiquity. The conflation of myth and the remote past produces a text that has had enduring influence on much later writers, including Wagner and Tolkien (see Byock 1990: 1–2 and again at 16–19). Indeed, due to the connection with Wagner in particular, Jesse L. Byock is prompted to gloss this saga with reference to the *Nibelungenlied*, while he observes that, by comparison, *The Saga of the Volsungs* has "[...] far fewer chivalric elements than its German counterpart" (Byock 1990: 4). This is important for three reasons. Firstly, it recognises that the *Nibelungenlied* is not a Germanic epic, but a romance. Secondly, as a romance, the south German text belongs to a different kind of Christianised culture from the saga; and thirdly, it explains why Wagner was drawn to the saga to round out the pagan elements of his Ring cycle, which turns out to be heavily Norse-influenced as a result.

In his narrative overview of the poem, Byock carefully delineates all of the important elements (8–11). As is common in the sagas, *The Saga of the Volsungs* has a two-part structure. The first part is mythic, concerning the legend of Sigurd's relationship to various supernatural beings and items, including a sword that needs to be reforged and a cursed ring, and the figure of Odin is particularly important in this part of the story. The second part of the saga deals with Sigurd's life and death in human society, after he joins the Burgundians through marriage. Here again it is kinship relations that provide the impetus for the main character's destruction. Byock provides a largely hypothetical historical context for the saga (11–16), including the often noted possibility that Sigurd (Siegfried in the *Nibelungenlied*) could be based on Arminius, the German leader who destroyed four Roman legions in the Teutoburger Wald during the reign of the emperor Augustus. This view cannot be fully supported, but it provides a point of comparison with Arthurian epic texts that are based on partial memories of a folk hero. The emergence of written forms based on such memorialisations underpins the saga form as a whole.

THE CELTS: TALES FROM IRELAND AND WALES

The American translator and critic Jeffrey Gantz entitles his Penguin Classics volume of Irish works *Early Irish Myths and Sagas* (Gantz 1981). Gantz labels Irish heroic tales as sagas, although he does not explain why he chooses to do so. At the very least, his selection of nomenclature implies some distance between the Irish material and continental European epic, but his use of the term "saga" suggests that even though Irish culture is different from that of the Norse-Icelandic world, the two do have some elements in common. There may be a historical reason for this, since much of Ireland was colonised by the Vikings, particularly around Dublin, and this may have led to the various story cycles eventually surviving in literary form. The earliest extant manuscripts date from the twelfth century and the Irish Christian culture that translated the stories into writing was similar to that of Iceland. However, such effects of cultural exchange are notoriously difficult to pin down where corroborating historical evidence is hard to find. Therefore, it may be more fruitful to consider Gantz's use of the term to refer to structural or typological similarities and to its implicit acknowledgement of differences from descendants of the Greek and Latin epic tradition.

First, however, it is crucial to note that Irish history is longer than that of Iceland, even if it is difficult to recreate. The various waves of migration into Ireland created a multivalent patchwork of myths, legends and pseudo-history, which is further complicated by the fact that the Celts did not in the first instance write

down their own versions of events. Gantz even goes so far as to
state that "[...] some elements must predate the arrival of the
Celts in Ireland" (Gantz 1981: 1–2), although of course if this
is true, any survivals are inevitably filtered through the world
view of the Celts who eventually became known as the Irish.
As Gantz observes, the haziness that results contributes to the
creation of a legendary world in which boundaries are permeable:

> Their setting is both historical Ireland (itself an elusive entity) and the
> mythic otherworld of the Side (Ireland's 'faery people', who live in
> burial mounds called 'side' and exhibit magical powers), and it is not
> always easy to tell one from the other. Many of the characters are
> partially euhemerized gods – that is, they are gods in the process
> of becoming ordinary mortals – so that, again, it is not easy to tell
> divine from human.
>
> (Gantz 1981: 1–2)

The faery world of the Side may well be a partial memory of
earlier peoples, but its relative proximity to the social world
of the Irish heroes suggests a clear difference from the under-
worlds commonly found in Greek epic. This alternative reality,
which can nevertheless be accessed from 'our' world, has important resonances for later literature such as Spenser's *The Faerie
Queene*. Similarly, the semi-divine origins of major characters
within the Irish tradition such as Cú Chulaind provide a point of
contact with epics from many other cultures.

As with the sagas, the Irish tales exhibit fewer and fewer
fanciful or mythological elements the closer they get to the
moment of writing. Gantz notes a provisional distinction between
the earliest, or mythological phase on the one hand, and the
pseudo-historical Ulster Cycle on the other (Gantz 1981: 7–8).
The former is characterised by interaction with the Side, and
often relates directly to seasonal or agricultural deities. Thus, in
The Wooing of Etain, love rivalry works as a *motif* for the seasonal
regeneration of fertility. *The Destruction of Da Derga's Hostel* carries
undertones of the death of a king and the end of summer, since
it is set at the feast of Samuin. *The Cattle Raid of Froech* is a
kind of transitional story, moving from the mythological to the

semi-historical world of the Ulster Cycle. These later stories are fuelled by the conflict between Ulster and Connacht, and Gantz uses the term 'saga' in conjunction with this second grouping, perhaps because these stories most closely approximate the Norse-Icelandic *milieu*. One feature that Gantz also notes is the disjunction between regal power and heroic prowess:

> Curiously, the kings of the Irish stories are not battle leaders: either they betray vestiges of divinity (Cú Ruí, for example) or they have a young champion as heir and rival. Examples of this second pattern – which reflects the relationship of Agamemnon to Achilles and anticipates those of Arthur to Lancelot and Mark to Tristan – are legion.
>
> (Gantz 1981: 9)

He goes on to ascribe exactly this relationship to Conchubur and Cú Chulaind in Ulster, and also their enemies King Ailill and his champion Cet. One might also add the relationship between Yudhishthira and his brothers in the *Mahabharata* to this list, or that between the Kings of Persia and Rustam in the *Shah-Namah*. The observation is an important one, since as Gantz's examples indicate, these details resonate very clearly with other epic cycles. In the Irish case, this doubled characterisation may have its roots in the originally sacral nature of kingship, as a marriage with the land reminiscent of the myth of the Fisher King. Whatever the antecedents, the structure offers great potential for both partnership and conflict between the king and the champion, a tension that will be greatly exploited in chivalric romance. Even when the king is represented as having been a great warrior in his own right, his deeds are often placed in the past. The Arthurian legends will repeat this temporal structure, although even in modern popular culture very little remains of the stories in which Arthur himself triumphs over various enemies. Instead, the various quests undertaken by his knights and, ultimately, the destruction of Camelot are much more marked. The mythic roots of all of these associations should be stressed, although at the same time it must be recognised that the ways in which these various narratives and legends influence and impinge upon one another will never fully be unravelled.

Indeed, charting the transmission and migration of narratives becomes doubly difficult when taking into account the disparate groups of Welsh stories that constitutes *The Mabinogion* (Gantz 1976), especially since the earliest manuscript copies of some of the tales date back as far as 1325.

The various moments of textual production incorporate elements of both past and present into the half-remembered, as opposed to selectively recalled, oral tales, a manoeuvre that replicates the procedure adopted in epic more generally, for example in narratives such as *Beowulf*. Further comparisons can be adduced with the *Shah-Namah,* the Irish works, and the sagas, since the earliest stories in *The Mabinogion* seem more myth-based than the later ones. This is especially true for the so-called Welsh romances in which figures from Arthurian tradition make their appearance (see Gantz 1976: 11). Due to the paucity of surviving manuscript materials, it cannot be said for certain that the three stories of Owein, Peredur and Gereint pre-date the continental Arthurian tradition, or indeed vice versa. A third possibility, of course, is the tempting one that the pseudo-Celtic Welsh stories and the romance tradition that finds its fullest expression in Chrétien de Troyes feed off one another. Though difficult to prove, this final suggestion has the advantage of taking geography into account, since the Brythonic proximity of Brittany, Cornwall and Wales suggests that there may have been occasions for narrative interplay, a cross-fertilising of various mythic and romance stories between different communities. This would explain the famously anachronistic intrusion of high medieval elements such as the knightly joust into a pagan Celtic past.

The Welsh stories, being Celtic half-memories, share certain features with the Irish narratives that have been discussed, and for similar reasons. Gantz covers many of these *motifs* in his Introduction to *The Mabinogion*, elements such as the importance of seasonal regeneration, euhemerisation and sacral kingship (Gantz 1976: 14–24), and he charts the overall historical development of the Arthurian *corpus*:

> These considerations offer some clue as to the development of the Welsh story, out of an ambience similar to that of the

Cú Chulaind tales to one more nearly approximating the Romances of Crestiens.

(Gantz 1976: 24)

Although he does not theorise it as such, Gantz is here ascribing a crucial liminal position to the Welsh tales, which would be supported by the underlying geographical links. In his introductory comments to *Pwyll Lord of Dyfed*, he adopts a comparative approach that permits him to refer not only to the Irish story of *The Wasting Sickness of Cú Chulaind*, but also to the intrusion of chivalric elements into the Welsh version. Additionally, he extends the scope of his comparison to recall Odysseus' reclaiming of Penelope on his return home in Homer's *Odyssey* (Gantz 1976: 45). Furthermore, he also suggests that *Branwen Daughter of Llŷr* "is an early and primitive version of the Grail legend" (66). When he introduces *How Culhwch Won Olwen*, Gantz offers a particularly interesting observation concerning the historical process that produced the Arthurian myth when he claims that:

Arthur, in what is probably his earliest appearance in Welsh prose, has a disappointingly minor role; already established as the great king of the British, he displays little personality. While the exploits which made him king lie in the Celtic past, the distinguishing characteristics which made him famous seem to lie in the continental future.

(Gantz 1976: 134–5)

In other words, Arthur may be a great King of Britain according to Celtic legend, but the narrative interest lies elsewhere, even this early in his textual career. The situation here recalls the Irish double structure of king as distinct from champion and this structure will continue into the romance versions of the Arthurian legend, and can be seen in the tale of *Owein, or The Countess of the Fountain* as it is presented in *The Mabinogion*. As Gantz realises, "'Owein' and 'Gereint' are actually mirror opposites of the same theme: the hero's knightly obligations balanced against his devotion to his lady" (Gantz 1976: 192). It would be difficult to find a more condensed statement of the *ethos* of romantic courtly love and, of course, what is crucial here is what it missing from the story (or, perhaps, taken for granted): the figuration of Arthur the King provides the context within which other heroes conduct their exploits. Further correspondences could be traced here with the Iliadic structure of the leader king Agamemnon and the great hero Achilles, the posture adopted by Yudhishthira in the *Mahabharata* relative to the fighting prowess of his brothers, and the status of Rustam in the *Shah-Namah*.

EPIC AND THE *CHANSONS DE GESTE*

The Old French epic poems known collectively as the *Chansons de Geste* follow the familiar pattern of epic composition. Many of them originate in popular culture, as oral tales that are recited or sung to music, and they become part of the repertoire of professional itinerant entertainers, while the written versions date from several centuries later. They recall events around the time of the reign of Charlemagne, but with a very definite feudal gloss, and they stand separate from the development of romance, with its emphasis on courtly love, although elements of each inform the other, especially by the thirteenth century. The most well-known is the *Song of Roland*, a text that Michael Newth links to the process of oral composition, while at the same time considering it to be the prime example of the literary genre as we have it:

> [...] the masterly level of sustained Epic diction achieved in the *Chanson de Roland*, the earliest complete written *chanson de geste* that we possess today, reflects and consummates a long legacy of prior oral composition within the genre.
>
> (Newth 2005: vii–viii)

According to Glyn S. Burgess, editor of the Penguin edition, the manuscript was probably written somewhere between 1130 and 1170, since it evinces Anglo-Norman features and is marked by recent and contemporary events, especially the onset of the First Crusade at the end of the eleventh century. This major historical event influences the work so much that its representations of the reign of Charlemagne suggest Christianity on the offensive (Burgess 1990: 8). In the narrative, Roland dies leading the rear-guard of Charlemagne's army as it returns across the Pyrenees after a successful campaign in Spain. The crusading influence can be seen in the way the poem changes the enemy from opportunistic Basque raiders to "Saracen" unbelievers, and Burgess notes: "This change permits the clash to be raised to the status of a struggle between Christians and pagans" (Burgess 1990: 10). It should also be realised that the poem's conception of exactly who these Saracens are is unclear, there being no real detailed awareness of their religious beliefs.

The poem's main set-pieces encapsulate the feudal concerns of its aristocratic readership (as opposed to the audiences who experienced it in oral form). Stanzas 8–26 show Charles (i.e. Charlemagne) in council, debating with his peers the next steps in the Spanish campaign. The episode is an important focus for political and ethical anxiety, because the discussion is grounded in a struggle between what is expedient, and what is right according to feudal codes of behaviour. Roland's stepfather, Ganelon, opposes him, and wins the argument thus introducing a second crucial element: kinship conflict, which is shown to be incompatible with feudal loyalties. The famous battle in which Roland is killed (stanzas 66–177) is not the climactic point of the poem as a whole, which continues the struggle against a hazily conceived Islamic enemy for another 121 stanzas. It is clear, therefore, that *The Song of Roland* is not just about Roland himself, but condenses a whole range of familial and feudal obligations into a story form that uses the figure of Roland to epitomise a much wider range of social and religious concerns, as Burgess observes: "The text is permeated by feudal terminology, feudal gestures, feudal attitudes" (Burgess 1990: 25), so much so indeed, that the hero Roland is less of a singular personage, but more a representative figure, constructed by the society of which he is a part.

Social constructs change precisely because they are sensitive to social change and this is especially true within the context of an evolving genre such as the *Chansons de Geste*. The history of the form demonstrates that it is capable of adaptation in the face of the emergence of its competitor, romance, and indeed the later *chansons* appropriate some of the elements of romance fiction; as Newth observes:

> Episodes of romance were included in response to the growing popularity of the 'tales of courtly love', of Breton lay and Arthurian legend, which the more literate and literary aristocracy wished increasingly to read privately, and not hear publicly.
>
> (Newth 2005: ix).

There is the suggestion here of a significant socio-historical movement that will eventually produce a literate and 'courtly' elite, a long process that is charted by the German cultural historian Norbert Elias in his book *The Court Society* (Elias 1983). He notes how courtly behaviour only occasionally manages to contain feudal violence:

> So the self-restraint which the *courtois* knights observe at court is only slightly consolidated into half-unconscious habits, into the almost automatic pattern characteristic of a later age.
>
> (Elias 1983: 261)

This formulation almost exactly describes the behaviour that takes place in the court and warfare situations that are depicted in *The Song of Roland*, although of course the historical period that the poem depicts pre-dates the court society explored by Elias. An almost automatic pattern of self-restraint, difficult to sustain in the poem itself, comes at a much later historical juncture.

A sophisticated literary form such as the *Chansons de Geste* registers an interplay of cultural elements to provide a multi-faceted narrative. As the *chansons* develop, their narratives change to accommodate the tastes of different audiences, and this can be traced in what Newth identifies as a range of details that extend the poems' appeal to non-aristocratic audiences (Newth 2005: x). Multiple viewpoints are expressed through different forms of stock characterisation, such that the 'official' version of the world of the knights is juxtaposed with that of lower social types designed to cater for differing audience tastes and expectations. These are early manifestations of the character types that evolve into the stock comic figures of later medieval and Renaissance drama, and who are the focus of the upside-down world of inverted official values. Additionally, such figures can be incorporated into literary versions, as can be seen in *The Song of William*:

> Most scholars agree that the *Chançun de Willame* proper ends at line 1980 of the surviving manuscript, and that the remaining 1574 lines, relating principally to the exploits of a kitchen-boy of royal blood called Renewart, are a scribal addition, probably folkloric in origin, and should be distinguished as the *Chançun de Rainouart*.
>
> (Newth 2005: 39)

Here we have a text in which the principle of comic inversion is applied by a highly literate copyist. Additionally, the second part of the *Song of William* has components that would seem to be influenced by romance, where narratives multiply and are fuller in terms of detail, where descriptions increase in volume, and where more attention is given to matters of characterisation (Newth 2005: 39). As a genre, then, the *Chansons de Geste* is marked by permeability to multiple outside influences. Newth contends that *Charlemagne's Pilgrimage* is a very specific satire upon the behaviour of Louis VII in the Second Crusade (Newth 2005: 146–7), and the critical stance that this implies is extended further in the group of *chansons* known as the cycle of rebellious barons (Newth 2005: 179). The model here is one of a political challenge to royal power that provokes a backlash from a centralising monarch.

The mutability of central control, and its phases of relative powerlessness followed by powerful reaction, is extremely important for the quest form so familiar from the romances. It is also possible to find in the *Chansons de Geste* a response to the structure of an enabling central authority that does not fight on its own behalf. In *The Knights of Narbonne*, six of the seven sons of Aymeri of Narbonne go on various quests, and their ensuing adventures are described in great detail. Descriptions of luxurious objects abound, as do travel sequences, both of which are features common in many other epic traditions. However, the superabundance of details of luxury and travel as *topoi* in themselves in *The Knights of Narbonne* marks this particular text as heavily influenced by romance. One reason for this is that in romance, the details are often elaborated as elements of interest in and of themselves, without necessarily advancing the action; also, the focus on courtly behaviour becomes more intense. However, it is important to remember that romance as a genre is contemporaneous with Old French epic in the form of the *Chansons de Geste*.

EPIC AND ROMANCE

In the same way that it is difficult to untangle romance features from epic poems, so too it is hard to distinguish epic elements from aspects of romance. A case in point is *The Nibelungenlied* (Edwards 2010), perhaps the best-known poem from the Middle High German period, not least because of the ways in which it has been appropriated by later cultures. Written down around 1200 CE, its obscure oral prehistory marks it as an epic work, as Cyril Edwards observes:

> *The Nibelungenlied* owes its origins to oral poetry. For a long time, for some five centuries if not more, the ancient tales to which the poet refers in the first strophe had been circulating in oral form, and we cannot be certain when they first made their entry into writing. These origins colour not only the plot and ethos, but also the lay's style.
>
> (Edwards 2010: xviii)

The situation here is broadly similar to the history as well as the content of the *Saga of the Volsungs*, both of which are rooted in the same mythic and pseudo-historical materials. Indeed, Edwards notes in his Introduction to the Oxford World Classics edition that "[…] there are echoes of an older, more heroic world, particularly in the second part of the lay" (Edwards 2010: xvi). Like the saga version, *The Nibelungenlied* has a two-part structure. The first part concerns the legendary deeds of Sigvit (more often denoted as 'Siegfried' in other editions), and the second deals with the aftermath of his death as his bereaved wife Kriemhilt sets out to avenge him. There are supernatural elements in both halves, such as Kriemhilt's dream of an eagle being killed by two falcons at the start of the main part of the narrative, and the prophecy of her vengeance in the second part of the poem. Such elements, however, are mostly to be found in the first half, the story of Sigvit, again offering a parallel with the *Saga of the Volsungs*. However, it is the historical moment at which the literary version is produced that marks the later work indelibly as a romance. Edwards describes the courtly *milieu* that informs the saga (Edwards 2010: xvi), and observes that despite its epic/heroic antecedents, the literary version is identifiable as a south German courtly romance; this is signalled by Edwards' constant use of the term 'lay', harking back to the Breton lays of Marie de France and thus, by association, to the romance traditions.

The legacy of the Welsh and Irish tales is also evident in *The Nibelungenlied*. Edwards notes that the relationship between King Gunther and Sigvit is a direct parallel with that between King Arthur and his knights (Edwards 2010: xiv). Here, however, kingship is distinguished from the martial heroism that Chretien inherits from the Celtic tales via Brittany, which he then proceeds to extend and refine. For example, *The Story of the Grail* is centred very much on the figure of Perceval; his deeds and piety may be occasioned by Arthur as king, but the narrative interest is on the prowess of the knight, not on an overarching royal authority. Once again, a familiar epic pairing of governing king and heroic war leader can be discerned.

The figure of Marie de France constitutes an important element of this process. The Breton lays ascribed to her represent a transitional form, incorporating various elements from troubadour poetry and Breton Celtic songs and stories. Even though most of these are not Arthurian, it is around this particular figure that the disparate components coalesce over time into a culturally resonant composite. As Glyn S. Burgess and Keith Busby note in the Preface to their second Penguin edition: "*Lanval* is Marie's only truly Arthurian lay and it has English analogues in the form of *Sir Launfal* and *Sir Landevale*" (in France 2003: 6). For a work to have analogues, it must form part of a network of migrating narratives. These are similar enough to produce multiple works in various languages, and they all relate to one another in complex ways. The geographical and cultural location of Brittany plays a crucial part in these shifts of emphasis, but similarity is not the same as identity, since the narrative trajectories change as they migrate.

Burgess and Busby are sensitive to differences between this tradition on the one hand, and that of the epic on the other, and they argue that:

> One basic distinction that can be made between the *lais* and the other Old French genres discussed so far which may well be at the root of the differences is that scholars generally regard the *lais* as belonging to what is known as 'courtly' literature and the epic and religious-didactic literature not.
>
> (Burgess and Busby in France 2003: 24)

This is an important observation, because it registers that in the late twelfth century courtly literature can still be distinguished from other narrative forms, although it is not an easy distinction to maintain (France 2003: 24). What is clear is that despite their complexity, and their inclusion of details of the supernatural (Burgess and Busby in France 2003: 33–4), there is a sense in which these works feed into other elements of the courtly *milieu*, and so cannot simply be treated in isolation. Moreover, Burgess and Busby imply in their reference to *The Allegory of Love* by C.S. Lewis (1938) that the emphasis placed by Lewis on allegory and courtly love is overstated; rather, they see allegory as only one element among others in the literature of this period. The critical point for which Lewis' work on romance is most famous is his contention that allegorical romance is the single most important literary form of the Middle Ages, and that all others are subordinate to it in status. Critics such as Burgess and Busby remind us that such a position can be criticised for being overly simplistic, especially when the continuing importance of epic is taken into account.

Chrétien de Troyes is equally influenced by the same combination of factors as Marie de France. However, there are also other considerations, the most important of which is the influence on Chrétien of Geoffrey of Monmouth's important and fanciful history of Britain's kings, the *Historia Regum Britanniae* (written around 1136). The story of Arthur takes up the whole of Books IX and X of Geoffrey's work, and spills over into Book XI. It includes the peculiar episodes in which Arthur defeats a Roman Emperor named Lucius and also fights a whole series of battles against Saxons and Normans. A contemporary of Marie de France, according to William W. Kibler:

> Chretien fashioned a new form known today as courtly romance. To Geoffrey's bellicose tales of Arthur's conquests, Chretien added multiple love adventures and a courtly veneer of polished manners.
>
> (Kibler in Troyes 2004: 1)

As Kibler observes, the *Chansons de Geste* reinterpret the Carolingian Empire for later French readers and audiences, just as Chrétien represents the world of Arthur through the *motifs* associated with contemporary chivalric discourse. For example, during the course of the narrative of *Erec et Enide*, a possible contradiction emerges between the demands of military life upon the knight and his fidelity to his beloved wife, a problem that the poem attempts to resolve by means of the romance quest. An alternative might be to discern a conflict between two social requirements: the dynastic imperative, and the call to action. Both are masculine in this society, but they are not always in harmony. Interestingly, it is Enide's intervention that sets in motion the romance narrative that will lead to a resolution, but only after a series of wandering encounters. Even though it is Enide who occasions the action, she is still circumscribed by her position as a woman, such that the patriarchy that underpins the romance acts by and through an appropriate (and appropriated) femininity. The image of the knight errant accompanied by his lady is an ideologically motivated convention that recapitulates the epic associations of the journey, but unlike the situation in the *Odyssey* for example, there is no prime importance accorded to the hero's homecoming, since his beloved travels with him.

Chrétien is well aware that he is working with conventions. Kibler's observation that "[...] scholars today often find in *The Knight of the Cart* extensive irony and humour, which serve to undercut the courtly love material" (in Troyes 2004: 8) is a reminder that this culture, including the poets themselves, was well aware of the artificiality of romance narratives. To recall the comments made earlier in relation to Norbert Elias, the world of romance has very little to do with the real existence of the feudal aristocracy; it is an idealising fiction, and the projected audiences and readers are certainly aware of this fact.

This observation points to a very sophisticated reading culture that is able to appreciate narrative complexity, including and especially the growing importance of allegorical elements where there is a creative interplay between form and content. A good example occurs in *The Knight with the Lion*, in which the wandering hero encounters a lion that embodies the knightly virtues. Historically speaking, knights either marched under the banner of a feudal lord, or they assumed the role of robber barons in their own right, imposing themselves violently on a vulnerable community. Marvellous adventures were the product of creative imaginations engaged in displacing 'reality' into fictional forms by according symbolic value to existing symbols of superiority and courage such as lions. The romances portray a series of encounters that enable the feudal aristocracy to see exalted and idealised versions of itself. In this respect, romance enacts a shift from epic to a form that addresses powerful social groups rather than a whole community.

In his edition, Kibler shows how allegory becomes more and more prominent as the Arthurian *oeuvre* matures, and he addresses particularly the allegorical issues surrounding *The Story of the Grail* and its Celtic roots (in Troyes 2004: 9–11). At the very least, this particular poem epitomises many of the complexities that lie at the heart of the romance form, especially those involving the association of courtly behaviour and the supernatural. The ascription of the Christianised knightly quest to an originally pagan Celtic story of the cup of the goddess permits the fusion of the narrative with the contemporary *ethos* from within which the poet is writing, but in allegorically displaced

forms that mediate the brutal realities of contemporary aristocratic behaviour.

The cultural influence of romance was considerable, including
its effect on the trajectory of epic, but it should not be
overestimated. Separate forms such as the epic *Chansons de Geste*
continued to flourish, but because their boundaries were permeable, they were able to appropriate romance elements.
Additionally, romance should not be treated as entirely homogeneous, since there are also variations within romance itself,
as can be seen in *Sir Orfeo,* the Middle English version of the
legend of Orpheus and Eurydice. Elaine Treharne has observed
that the inscription of a happy ending permits this poem to
avoid excessive allegorising of the kind imposed on the story by
Boethius (Treharne 2010: 551), and she is careful to point out
that romance cannot simply be reduced to allegory. The particular example of *Sir Orfeo* challenges generalisation, and this is
typical of other texts of the period. The continued existence of
epic forms and the variations that are produced within romance
would suggest that the allegorical *trope*, powerful though it may
be, is utilised primarily for practical purposes. Treharne notes
the debt that this poem owes its Breton antecedents, but
she is also careful to point out its Celtic roots, especially in the
figuration of an underworld that is in fact an alternative reality
(Treharne 2010: 551), one that continues to exist beyond the
formal restoration of order at the end of the poem. *Sir Orfeo* dates
from the heyday of romance, written in the early fourteenth
century, and is fully influenced by the Breton and French
tradition. However, not all Middle English literature is quite so
self-conscious in the way that *Sir Orfeo* pulls together details from
different traditions. The most well-known of the romances is
probably *Sir Gawain and the Green Knight*, which encapsulates the
romance world of Arthurian legend without necessarily calling it
into question. These modulations demonstrate the transformations
that the *ethos* associated with epic undergoes as a result of incor-
poration into a range of medieval forms.

A particular case in point is the first two of *The Canterbury Tales*
(Chaucer 2003), *The Knight's Tale* and *The Miller's Tale*. At
first sight the priority given to *The Knight's Tale* seems to give

it pre-eminence among the individual stories, coming as it does immediately after the Prologue. It subsequently attracted many imitators, forming the basis for the collaborative play *The Two Noble Kinsmen* by Fletcher and Shakespeare, among others, but Chaucer's version is itself intertextual, based on Boccaccio's *Teseida*, a long segment of which is devoted to the fight between two knights over the Lady Emilia. The Italian and English texts articulate a standard romantic placement of courtly characters within the court of Theseus. Hence the conflation of the para- phernalia of medieval romance (jousts, courtly love) with the pre-Christian world of the classical gods and goddesses. Arcite wins the ritual combat because he prays to Mars, while Palamon ultimately gains Emily because he prays to Venus. The *ethos* of Christian romance displaces the violence of pagan epic because love must triumph over all, even if the knight prays to a pagan goddess.

This story, replete with its cultural markers in epic violence and the moralising of romance, is followed immediately by its undoing in the form of *The Miller's Tale*, which punctures the chivalric ideology by offering a more 'realistic' account of love (and lust). Although the characters are from an inferior social class compared to that described by the Knight, the satirical attack on the *ethos* of courtly love is clear. By undercutting the world of romance, the Miller exposes its ideological content and, in the best traditions already seen in the *Chansons de Geste*, he ultimately gets away with it because he is drunk. The *Canterbury Tales* con- tinue, of course, which means that the conflict laid bare by these two initial stories is left unresolved: readers are simply given one version of love, followed by another, and then left to make up their own minds, a different situation from the resolution demanded by epic narrative strategies.

EPIC AND ALLEGORY

Despite the variety and the dispersal of its associated forms, there are certain common elements and techniques that epic shares with other genres. One of the most obvious is allegory as it operates within the courtly romance, but also because it facilitates connections with religious iconography and poetry. In the writings of the Italian poet Dante the two come together because of the importance he attaches to idealised love. In the *Divine Comedy* (written between 1308–21), the poet ultimately makes use of his deceased ideal beloved Beatrice, who becomes a means of ascent to a vision of heaven, but a great deal of struggle has to take place before this resolution is reached. Dante manages his narrative progression through a dynamic combination of the epic form and contemporary religious allegory, and this allows him to demonstrate his mastery both of form and *motif* in an epic poem that is resolutely literary.

The beginning of the *Divine Comedy* signals exactly these issues by means of a very specific narrative invention:

> Midway upon the journey of our life
> I found myself within a forest dark,
> For the straightforward pathway had been lost.
>
> (Dante 2010: *Inferno* I.1.1–3)

Dante manages his epic by figuring himself as the main character of the poem, a pilgrim, and this poetic self-consciousness takes the logic of narrative unity to a new level, which Dante regards as a development of the classical epic tradition from Homer, through Virgil, to his own times. This strategy accounts for the importance of Virgil as a guiding influence in the first half of the poem, both metaphorically and literally, and the combination of authorial persona plus classical predecessor permits a duality of narrative expression. The pilgrim narrates his experiences first-hand, while the guiding figure glosses them, thereby setting up standards of judgement at the level both of form, as he reworks the epic as a genre, and content, which he explicitly Christianises. The pilgrim's journey through purgatory and hell and on up to heaven recasts an epic narrative *motif* that has a long history.

Moments of allegorical meaning emerge throughout the poem, often mediated by the guide; for example, at *Purgatorio* I.32.2, Virgil ties a reed girdle around Dante's waist, just after the two have emerged from hell and are about to go up the mountain of purgatory, which is itself divided into seven parts corresponding to the seven deadly sins. The reed (which suggests Palm Sunday) is meant to ward off the worst of these, pride, from which all other deadly sins spring. At *Purgatorio* IX.26.1–2, Dante and Virgil find three different coloured stairs leading up to a doorway that is guarded by an angel. According to the translator Henry Longfellow's gloss on this Canto, these three steps symbolise "the three parts of penitence – confession, contrition and satisfaction" (in Dante 2010: 196). The poem is simply saturated with moments like these, with almost every encounter and every description imbued with a carefully elaborated symbolic meaning.

The central force of the poem is the idealised love of God, and Virgil is given the first opportunity to expound its importance at *Purgatorio* XV.16–27. He tells Dante that Beatrice will be his guide as he moves steadily towards heaven, but he continues to declaim on love at *Purgatorio* XVII, relating it to the doctrine of the seven deadly sins by means of a series of exemplars drawn from biblical and classical literature. Even though as a non-Christian Virgil cannot himself be fully admitted to heaven, as a poet he is the ideal person initially to convey the importance of this location. The linkage with poetry is continued at *Purgatorio* XXIV, when Dante meets one of his Florentine fellow poets, and again at *Purgatorio* XXVI. However, this is as far as mortal poetry can take him, the allegorical point being that direct beneficence of divine grace is needed before the mortal soul can proceed any further. This is the point at which the non-Christian Virgil is replaced as guide by the Christian Beatrice, which signals that the religious *ethos* of Dante's poem replaces, and is superior to, the temporal imperialism of the *Aeneid*. Both poems are concerned with the imperatives placed on the individual by a greater power than himself. In the case of the *Aeneid*, this is the divine plan that requires Aeneas to tear himself away from Dido and found Rome, a dedication to a mission that the poem encompasses in terms of its concept of *pietas*. For Dante, a different kind of piety demands that the pilgrim subordinate himself to the exigencies of Christianity.

Placing emphasis on poetry produces another advantage, in that it enables Dante to position his own work in explicit relation to his classical forebears, and to situate the *Divine Comedy* within a dynamic context that it both enhances and extends. This matters because Dante is using the vernacular to reinvent the epic, in much the same way that his predecessor had appropriated the form for Latin, so that the shadow of Virgil accompanies Dante in more ways than one. However, since the pagan poets are clearly shown to be deficient because they are not Christians, Dante's new Italian epic is given enhanced status in relation to the past, in that the poem's Christian emphasis confers upon the epic a superior ethical position by comparison with its classical forebears.

The result is no mere antiquarianism. When Dante mentions historical or legendary figures, he often does so in relation to more recent Italian personages; for example, when Dante and Virgil descend to the Second Circle of Hell, they see the ghosts of famous lovers: Semiramis, Dido, Helen, Achilles and Paris from antiquity, together with Paolo Malatesta and Francesca da Rimini (*Inferno* V). Similarly, at *Inferno* XVIII they see Jason together with Venedico Caccianemico, one of Dante's political enemies from Florence. At *Inferno* XII, Dante sees a sculptural representation of the sin of pride showing Satan together with Briareus, Thymbraeus, Pallas, Mars, Nimrod, Niobe, Saul, Arachne and Rehoboam. These associations permit Dante to register his knowledge of the classical texts and at the same time add to an expanding catalogue of references that reinforces the kinship with epic form.

The inclusion of Capaneus (*Inferno* XIV) is particularly interesting, since Statius joins Virgil and Dante as a secondary guide at *Purgatorio* XXI. The mountain of purgatory has just released him to fly upwards to the heavens after serving his time of penance. Here occurs one of those strange textual indications that Dante is very much a man of his time: he ascribes Statius' salvation (unlike the case of Virgil) to having become a secret convert to Christianity, which seems to have been a commonplace belief. Dante is able to introduce Statius personally to his poetic forebear, to whom he is indebted. It is easy at such a remove to forget how highly the *Thebaid* of Statius was regarded in the Middle Ages, particularly because of its subsequent eclipse by the *Aeneid*. In the next Canto Statius reveals that he has had to spend time in purgatory because he sinned in keeping his Christianity secret. Dante's poem therefore demonstrates his deep knowledge of the epic tradition, while at the same time it bears witness to the sheer unpredictability of the trajectory of intertextual relations.

The poem registers knowledge of Christian learning as much as it does of classical. The Eastern Roman Emperor Justinian appears at *Paradiso* VI and there is a veritable catalogue of Christian writers at *Paradiso* X. Dante makes another typical medieval error, however, when he sees the Emperor Trajan in heaven at *Paradiso* XX; in fact, Trajan's correspondence with Pliny the Younger had not yet been rediscovered. Here the emperor advises Pliny, governor of Bithynia-Pontus, to punish recalcitrant Christians, but not to pursue them, an important distinction because although Trajan does not want to persecute Christians, any who are brought before Pliny in his role as magistrate must be dealt with if they refuse to recant (Pliny 1968: 295).

The *Divine Comedy* is also saturated with references to Dante's own direct engagement with Florentine politics, allowing him to score points against his rivals. He takes advantage of his exile from Florence to manipulate the events surrounding his own writing of the poem and his pilgrim persona hears several retrospectively constructed prophecies about the outcome of civil discord in his home city. A good example occurs when Ciacco bewails his punishment in hell for the sin of gluttony at *Inferno* VI.22–5. The thief Vanni Fucci makes the same kind of prediction at *Inferno* XXIV.48–50. At *Purgatorio* VI, Longfellow notes that "Dante starts to inveigh against the political factions keeping Italy divided and then launches into a savage and ironic criticism on Florence and its perpetual shifts of power" (in Dante 2010: 184).

Dante regards these changes of fortune as ethical and religious, but he emphasises that the affairs of the world are not devoid of moral context. In his short introduction to *Purgatorio* XVI, Longfellow writes:

> The spirit of Marco the Lombard guides the poets through the clouds as he outlines the political factors corrupting the world, plays

down the influences of fate on human affairs, affirms the divine
notion of free will and laments the lack of good political and religious
leaders.

(Longfellow in Dante 2010: 222)

Marco the Lombard stresses the central importance of the principle of free will, a further moment in the process of Christianising
the epic, and this is an important departure from the classical
tradition, where fate is a major deciding factor, above the power
of the gods. The result is, as Marco realises, the inability of
Italy to produce effective social and religious leadership. The
poem is here resolutely faithful to its *milieu*, as it registers a link
between religious and temporal power. This confluence is partly
the result of other powers interfering in Italian affairs, with the
result that the poem's scathing political critique is not limited to
Italy. In *Purgatorio* XX, Dante and Virgil encounter Hugh Capet,
who attacks his own descendants, the kings of France, for their
actions, while at *Paradiso* XX, the targets are Albert of Austria
and Philip IV of France.

Almost inevitably, Dante's attacks on politicians are also
extended to the corruption of the Church, to some extent as a
result of the Church's direct involvement in temporal affairs, since
the Papal States held political and military power in their own
right during this period. However, here Dante also registers
abuses of both temporal and sacerdotal power often noted by
many of his contemporaries. This is not to say that his is
a demotic epic, of the sort that appeared slightly later in *Piers
Plowman* in Middle English. Even so, religious critique is a
constant refrain in *The Divine Comedy*; for example, at *Inferno* XI.3,
Virgil and Dante come across the tomb of Pope Anastasius II, in
the Sixth Circle of Hell. *Inferno* XIX is particularly revealing
in this connection, when Dante encounters a series of popes con-
demned to live upside down with their legs sticking out of holes
in the bedrock of hell, making this Canto a particularly effective
excoriation of sinful Church practices. Hidden within it, however,
is a subtle indication of Dante's own political stance; the point of
reference to Clement V suggests that he was probably the pope in
power at the time of writing *The Divine Comedy*. Dante's (losing)

faction in Florence was opposed to a full extension of the temporal power of the papacy.

The most severe censure of Church corruption is reserved for the later parts of the poem, gathering force from *Purgatorio* XXXIII onwards. If anything, the attack intensifies in *Paradiso*, and it could be interpreted as an attempt by Dante to give his criticism celestial force. The Church and the pope as its head are supposed to shepherd Christians towards heaven, but here Dante has the inhabitants of heaven attacking religious abuses. At *Paradiso* XI, Saint Thomas Aquinas reveals to Dante that Saint Dominic and Saint Francis of Assisi (founders of monastic orders) have been mandated by heaven to renew the Church. Dante launches into extravagant praise of the latter in particular, but although both orders are accepted by the papacy, the impetus to renewal comes in the first instance from outside the officially sanctioned structure. The critique is repeated at *Paradiso* XXI, when the Benedictine Saint Peter Damian "denounces the indulgent lifestyle of prelates" (Longfellow in Dante 2010: 345). Longfellow's gloss here refers implicitly to the common medieval charges against the rich lives of bishops and cardinals, the princes of the Church. The well-known phrase itself elides associations of temporal power with the supposed religious role, and the attack builds to a crescendo as "Beatrice prophesies that Dante will live to see God's vengeance rain down on the Church's corrupters" (349). Ultimately, "St Peter flushes with anger as he denounces all the evil popes, declaring the papal see 'vacant'" (362).

All of these conflicting and competing energies have to be managed somehow and Dante does so through an authorial narrative that forms a bridge with the internal figure of the pilgrim. This marks his poem as resolutely and self-consciously literary since the intrusion of such a narrative voice is a marked development of the first person singular form that he inherited from the *Aeneid*, especially the poet's conventional invocation to the muse. But Dante extends the device, as we see in the following example:

> Reader, thou seest well how I exalt
> My theme, and therefore if with greater art

I fortify it, marvel not thereat.

(Dante 2010: *Purgatorio* IX.24)

The direct address to the reader involves him or her in a closed hermeneutic circle that involves collusion in the literary process, and it takes the form of a flattering invitation to follow the traces of Dante's art; it is a subtle compliment, since Dante's ideal reader will of course recognise every allusion and every movement of the poem's intricate progression. The authorial intervention is repeated at *Purgatorio* XXIX.33, the first of the allegorical masques already noted, while at *Paradiso* II.1–2 Dante says that any unprepared reader should stop reading at this point, because he is about to treat of matters of the highest importance.

Ultimately, such moments are indications of a sophisticated strategy of representation that extends the possibilities of epic form. The crux comes at the end of *Purgatorio*, at Cantos XXX–XXXI, when Virgil disappears and is replaced by Beatrice. This signals a move beyond the classical, as Dante enacts a Christian appropriation of the epic, and the *Divine Comedy* ends with the pilgrim gazing raptly upon the final divine mystery, one whose beauty and truth cannot be conveyed through mortal language:

O how all speech is feeble and falls short
Of my conceit, and this to what I saw
Is such, 'tis not enough to call it little!

(Dante 2010: *Paradiso* XXXIII.41)

The complex relationship between courtly forms such as the romance and the cultures for which it was written demonstrates that at the very least the epic is open to reconceptualisation. However, the process of change is not all in the one direction. Epic forms, techniques and narratives infiltrate other literary genres and it is this capacity for transformation that gives epic its vitality, even for periods that seem to be incapable of producing their own epics. The Renaissance will seek to extend epic form and content, taking the appeal of epic in new directions.

4

THE RENAISSANCE AND THE EARLY NOVEL

Many of the strands of epic and romance that have been traced in the 'Middle Ages' also come together unevenly during the Renaissance. They continue to react against one another in very specific ways, as narrative techniques and allegorical method intersect with each other. This produces a tension between historical material on the one hand and literary tradition on the other. There is also a further tension between the history that is to be represented and the moment of writing. Conflicting factors and the confluences they produce imbue the various texts with tensions and the result can seem, from a modern perspective, to be a radical speeding up of the migration of narratives. We have already noted the influence of narrative forms upon one another that is a feature of medieval texts, and in such circumstances it is worth recalling that epic is not a singular form at all. If we think of epic as a function in addition to its existence as a form, then we begin to glimpse its multiple potentialities. Regarded in this way, it can be thought of as a generic space.

One of the major peculiarities of Renaissance epic is its propensity to incompleteness. This may be a symptom, indeed a direct result, of the many incompatibilities that are thrown up in this period. Perhaps this is because at a formal level it becomes very difficult indeed for a poet to manage adequately all of the disparate elements of epic, romance and allegory. However, such a formulation may run the risk of locating the difficulties of Renaissance epic, as well as those produced by it, purely within the persona of the writer, when in fact there may well be wider historical factors at work. David Quint begins by describing in general the initial focus of his book on classical epic, and then diverges into a historicist analysis of the growing importance of the association of epic with the early modern European aristocracy. He argues that the role of the aristocracy comes under intense pressure from absolutist monarchy on the one hand, and competition for social prestige from the aggressive mercantile classes on the other (Quint 1993: 10). According to Quint's analysis, the Renaissance revival of epic by and for a sophisticated humanist aristocracy comes immediately prior to the eclipse of that nobility's power:

> Paradoxically, at the moment of absolutist ascendancy in the seventeenth century, when European monarchies were acquiring power in unprecedented concentrations, the epic poems that should have celebrated that power failed artistically. These very poems, along with other, more successful contemporary efforts at heroic poetry, looked back nostalgically to a nobility and valor not yet subject to royal control.

> (Quint 1993: 10)

Such historical changes clearly produce tensions that are elaborated in the literature that is associated with them. It should therefore be possible to discern in the Renaissance some of the elements that, to follow Quint's line of reasoning, will lead to the death of epic as a form associated primarily with the aristocracy.

THREE ITALIANS AND TWO ENGLISHMEN

It is relatively easy to trace a line of descent from Italian writers of epic such as Boiardo through Ariosto and Tasso to Edmund

Spenser, and the context is provided by exactly those shifting congruent elements of romance, epic and allegory that have already been noted. The result is a departure from the accepted 12-book structure to a more fluid, less easily contained and constrained format: that of a different number of books, each divided into a varying number of cantos. Metrically, the Italians abandoned the hexameter for the *ottava rima*, although the reason for this move away from the heavy metrical beat associated for so long with epic is unclear. However, it can be no coincidence that the change in metre occurs at more or less the same time as the change in structure. Such formal changes reflect a corresponding diversity in representational practice. One of the translators of Boiardo's *Orlando Innamorato*, Charles Stanley Ross, notes that:

> The *Innamorato* is not merely the precursor to one of the most celebrated poems in English. It is a great work of art in its own right, one of the supreme products of the Italian Renaissance; yet, almost contradictorily, the poem captures the waning of the Middle Ages. It gives sophisticated form to a simpler world of knights and ladies.
>
> (Ross in Boiardo 1995: viii)

If Ross' claim that supposedly simpler times are represented in a much more sophisticated form is aligned with David Quint's use of the term 'nostalgia', it becomes possible to detect an ideological impulse, as the later period seeks to re-present to itself a wholly imaginary world of knights and ladies whose primary existence is in literature. Boiardo's poem not only delineates the waning of the Middle Ages, but it also recaptures the waning of a literary version of a decline, producing, in short, a kind of retrospectively directed 'medievalism'.

Boiardo is particularly successful in producing this image. His poem fuses the Carolingian tradition familiar from the *Chansons de Geste* with the Arthurian *mythos*. He takes the romance elements of the latter and retrospectively invests the Carolingian court with courtly behaviour. The two genres had, of course, played off each other for centuries, but they come together to produce a new synthesis in Boiardo's *Orlando Innamorato*. His Orlando is a new version of Roland, who is in turn part of a whole series of imaginative revisions of Charlemagne's career. His court is made into a pseudo-Arthurian *milieu* of questing knights and adventures against Muslim/pagan adversaries, none of which is even remotely historically plausible, and it also becomes the *locus* for a courtly love that was previously the domain of Arthurian romance.

Boiardo's poem catches the historical moment, producing a host of associations that prove to be surprisingly powerful, and this is especially true of the female figures he depicts. It is almost as though the old romance stereotypes are given a new lease of life in this Renaissance form, as Ross observes:

> [...] indeed the *Innamorato* is famous for its enchantresses, figures like Dragontina, Falerina, Morgana, and Alcina. These women, some of whom continue the tradition of fays found in earlier French romances, inhabit a series of magic domains whose allegories have only recently been unveiled by scholars but whose influence on later literature, especially on Tasso's Armida, Spenser's Bower of Bliss, and their imitators, is a commonplace of literary history.
>
> (Ross in Boiardo 1995: viii)

The effects these figures have on the knights errant is not, how-ever, straightforward, since it is a result of the fusion of the two traditions. Indeed, one of the features that Ross goes on to identify is the discrepancy between them that provides great scope for humour in the *Innamorato* (in Boiardo 1995: xiii). The result is a whole series of wandering encounters in which the ends of epic are deferred by the conditions of romance. Orlando the great warrior turns into a fool for love as the story is modu-lated into what becomes a tripartite structure. He and various others pursue Angelica; there is a great siege at Albracca; and the Moors attack Paris and engage in a series of battles with Charlemagne's troops. Ultimately there is no resolution, since the poem remains unfinished.

Ariosto picks up the thread of the narrative where Boiardo leaves off, with the *Orlando Furioso* continuing the structure and the *ethos* of its predecessor. It has the same tripartite structure and the same intertwining of epic and romance elements, except that it intensifies the endless diversions characteristic of romance. The result is a poem that achieved even more popularity than Boiardo's, because Ariosto succeeded in inflecting the form with meanings that would appeal to his contemporary readers.

Guido Waldman places Ariosto very firmly in a series of social and political relations, with his suggestion that: "The Estes had a passion for the chivalric romances and the lost world they portrayed – the panoply of which they tried to recapture by staging jousts on gala occasions" (in Ariosto 2008: xii). The Italian dukes who patronised Ariosto therefore replay exactly the nostalgia to which David Quint draws our attention, and they are content to support client poets who pander to their predilection for chivalric romance. However, Quint also suggests that the *Orlando Furioso* represents a major development in the ongoing relationship between epic and romance. In particular, he associates a quasi-Dyonisiac desire with romance, suggesting that Ariosto's digressions, or eruptions of energy, are structurally opposed to the rational thrusting linearity of the epic master-narrative (Quint 1993: 38). His account is somewhat at odds with that of Waldman, who describes in some detail the main elements of *Orlando Innamorato* (in Ariosto 2008: xii–xiii), but who differentiates the earlier poem from *Orlando Furioso* on the grounds that the latter displays superior poetic and narrative skills (xiii–xiv). Waldman reduces the transition from Boiardo to Ariosto to the issue of differing poetic skill and narrative control, which is exactly what Quint claims is challenged by the potentially disruptive intrusion of romance elements into an otherwise linear narrative structure.

The intertextual relationship between Boiardo and Ariosto is replayed in different form between Ariosto and Tasso, the third of the major Italian Renaissance writers of romance. The initial version of Tasso's *Liberation of Jerusalem* was completed in 1574 and he closely followed the example of his two predecessors when producing his own narrative of romantic deviations. However, as Mark Davie notes in his Introduction to the poem, the context within which Tasso operated was significantly different from those of Boiardo and Ariosto (in Tasso 2009: xii). In particular, the publication of a Latin translation of Aristotle's *Poetics* in 1536 had led to changes in literary taste with the result that, despite its undoubted popularity, Tasso's poem became embroiled in a debate in which narrative unity was privileged, a neo-Aristotelian critical axiom that became popular with Elizabethan writers such as Sir Philip Sidney.

The result is a poem that was published in two distinct versions, the first of which contained elements that were much more aligned with romance rather than epic, and the second of which reversed this distinction. Tasso was acutely aware of the difficulties of combining romance with epic, and he tried to keep the former under (relative) control. This is partly explained by his location in a different historical and cultural era from his two predecessors; Tasso certainly reacted to some extent against the dubious personal morals of some of the knights in the Orlando stories, but unlike Boiardo and Ariosto, he chose a much more solid historical setting for his poem: the story of the First Crusade and the eventual conquest of Jerusalem. He is well aware that an important structural element of epic as it evolved was the overcoming of various obstacles, and these are provided by romance components such as Amida's garden (cantos 15–16), which act as counterpoints to the central (epic) story line. The poem's complex structure allows Tasso constantly to play epic and romance off against each other in a double movement that serves to direct the narrative towards the successful capture of Jerusalem. Thus, in this instance, romance is in theory at least subordinated to the exigencies of the epic.

However, the reality is far less clear than this ostensible resolution might suggest. The reason for this is that the narrative energies associated with romance are not so easily contained; in fact, they are often much more interesting and dynamic in their own right than the overall advancing plotline of the crusade appears to be. For example, the garden of Amida in cantos 15–16 is a direct descendant of the *motif* encountered in the story of Rustam in the *Shah-Namah* and will be replicated by Spenser in the Bower of Bliss episode at the end of Book II of *The Faerie Queene*. Thus, despite his protestations that he is in fact writing an epic, especially at the outset of *The Liberation of Jerusalem,* Tasso is as caught up in the same confusion of romance and epic as are

Boiardo and Ariosto, albeit in a different cultural context. Tasso's text is inevitably affected by the moralising impetus of the counter-reformation, ultimately leading him to publish a radically revised version of the poem in 1592, 12 years after he completed his original text. An old form is here being required to assimilate into itself new social pressures, so much so that Tasso clearly felt the need to issue a new version of the poem that revised and occasionally deleted many of its romance elements.

The Italian poets undoubtedly influenced Spenser's *The Faerie Queene,* which also deployed the multiple book and canto structure. Indeed, Spenser continued the move away from the rhythm of the iambic pentameter by adopting a specific stylistic innovation, that came to be called the 'Spenserian' stanza. However, there were also native British precursors of his poem, the most important of which was Sir Thomas Malory's prose collection of Arthurian narratives in English, *Le Morte d'Arthur* (Malory 2004). Malory's text was published in 1485 by Caxton, and as one of the first printed books in English, it belongs to the Renaissance, even though its romance material seem to indicate a close affinity with the medieval world. The categories are unclear, and it is the book's transitional status – coming as it does at the end of the Middle Ages and the beginning of the Renaissance – that makes it so important. Its content makes it nostalgic but its form makes it revolutionary. The publication date is itself significant, since 1485 was the year in which Richard III was defeated in battle, inaugurating the reign of the first Tudor monarch, Henry VII, and is often regarded as the historical moment that signalled the end of the medieval period in English history. Caxton divides his edition into 21 books, covering almost every conceivable aspect of Arthurian 'history'. It ranges from Arthur's own youthful heroic deeds through his military achievements as king on to the exploits of his knights, and culminating in the final catastrophe at the end of his reign. Strong mythological elements are a feature of much historical writing of this period, but although Malory tried to produce in his narrative some sort of pseudo-chronological order, the result was an inevitable unevenness. For example, the inclusion of the story of Arthur's conquest of Rome has no relation to the rest of the work, which is taken up with events within Britain. The cultural importance of his book, however, remains uncontested, and Stephen H.A. Shephard's edition includes a useful selection of secondary criticism that confirms its abiding appeal (in Malory 2004: 797–905). Malory's Arthurian collection ranks alongside the work of the Italian Renaissance poets, and collectively they exerted a major influence on English writers such as Edmund Spenser. For Spenser, Tasso is a ready-made source of moralising elements to be taken over for a particular project, the allegorical lionising of a Protestant queen. The poem that results covers some of the same ground as in Malory, although Spenser's impetus is a partial mythologizing of some of the exploits of Arthur and, in Book 1 of *The Faerie Queene*, St George.

The Faerie Queene follows Malory in returning the Arthurian *mythos* to Britain, but at the same time the moralising impetus behind Tasso's need to revise his work is also present in Spenser's poem. Thus, while indebted to earlier Italian examples, in terms of its *ethos*, *The Faerie Queene* is a resolutely Protestant work and this combination occurs at the same time as a nascent British Empire begins to emerge. Like its Italian precursors, Spenser's poem is incomplete, although its overall design is made clear in his own prefatory explanation:

> [...] I labour to pourtraict in Arthure, before he was king, the image of a brave knight, the which is the purpose of these first twelue books: which if I finde to be well accepted, I may be perhaps encouraged, to frame the other part of politicke vertues in his person, after that hee came to be king.
>
> (Spenser 1984: 16)

On the evidence of his dedicatory letter to Sir Walter Raleigh, who was himself to become a controversial aristocratic contemporary, it would seem that Spenser was anticipating a work of 24 books, divided into two sections of 12, with the second to be undertaken only if the first received critical acceptance. Each of the two subdivisions was intended to deal with 12 virtues, the second of which would be those associated with good governance. Each of the completed books consists of 12 cantos of the form that was made familiar by the texts of Boiardo, Ariosto and Tasso. In the event, Spenser completed only six books, three in 1590 and a further three in 1597, with a kind of *coda* in the form of the *Mutabilitie Cantos*, which emphasised the importance of an Ovidian acceptance of the mutability of human life and constant change.

To some extent, the lack of a structured conclusion to *The Faerie Queene* can be explained symptomatically to be a triumph of romance over epic. The sheer size of the project perhaps accounts for its unfinished state, but as with the Orlando poets, the material itself is, in and of itself, intractable and difficult to control. As David Quint argues, there is a conflict in the poem between Spenser's use of multiple romance plots and what appears to be an otherwise straightforward narrative of an imperial epic project (Quint 1993: 40). *The Faerie Queene* attempts to subordinate the wandering energies of romance to a very precise rendering of the imperialist impulse, and its intended unification of the whole of Britain under the aegis of Gloriana and Arthur is designed to provide the means to subsume the variety of cultures that exist elsewhere in the British Isles. This is especially true in the case of Ireland, where Spenser himself had particular colonial interests, and which is treated allegorically in Book 5. The colonisation of Ireland pre-dates the partial unification of England and Scotland that occurred when James VI of Scotland succeeded to the English throne as James I in 1603 and is an extension of an imperial impulse.

The poem's allegorical figures represent particular aspects of contemporary issues, and its narrative casts them in 'epic' terms. The plotline of each book deploys in large part a distinctly medieval romance narrative, although the object of the questing knights' attentions is ultimately Gloriana herself, identified with the reigning monarch, Elizabeth I. Various struggles lead to a crisis for the protagonists at the halfway mark, at which point the figure of Arthur or one of his proxies intervenes, and then leaves.

Book 1 deals with the virtue of holiness, and the hero is the crusading Redcrosse Knight, whose escutcheon, the red cross, is also the flag of St George, the patron saint of England. It is his task to escort the Lady Una to her homeland, which is under siege from a dragon. The iconography has a long Christian history and the dragon represents Satan attacking the true Church, while Una is a feminised representation of Protestant truth. This becomes very clear in the Wood of Error, when the Redcrosse Knight confronts a horrific beast in its den that in allegorical terms represents both the Catholic Church and a negative aspect of femininity in direct opposition to Una. As the following description makes clear, this beast is an instrument of Satan that threatens Protestant values:

> Therewith she spewd out of her filthy maw
> A floud of poyson horrible and blacke,
> Full of great lumpes of flesh and gobbets raw,
> Which stunk so vildly, that it forst him slacke
> His grasping hold, and from her turne him backe:
> Her vomit full of books and papers was,
> With loathly frogs and toades, which eyes did lacke,
> And creeping sought way in the weedy gras:
> Her filthy parbreake all the place defiled has.

(Spenser 1984: I.i.20)

In the martial combat that follows, Error represents the evils of the church of Rome, while the poisonous books and pamphlets that are spewed out are the products of the Catholic counter-reformation. This is the first in a series of encounters in Book 1 where Redcrosse Knight defeats the false doctrines of the Roman Catholic Church, variously characterised as the Whore of Babylon as an avatar of Satan, but before he can engage with the devil, he has to struggle against various false doctrines and personages who are the instruments of evil. Behind this historical struggle lies a series of archetypal conflicts, and Spenser makes sense of contemporary political and religious anxieties through a mode of representation that aligns these concerns with a heavily moralised and gender-stereotypical version of epic.

The first book sets the pattern for the events that follow: an overall major quest or journey composed of various trials leading up to a final climactic struggle. Book 2 deals with the virtue of

Temperance in the figure of the knight Guyon whose fortitude is tested in a similar manner to that of Redcrosse Knight. Just as the latter was exposed to the court of Lucifera, the female face of Satan (as her name suggests) and the Seven Deadly Sins in Book 1 (1.4), so Sir Guyon is exposed to unconstrained desire when he arrives at the Bower of Bliss, presided over by Acrasia. Sir Guyon responds in a characteristically violent manner to the Bower's temptations, and this has given some modern critics who are sympathetic to Freudian accounts of human behaviour cause for concern. For example, in a persuasive discussion of the episode in *Renaissance Self-Fashioning* (Greenblatt 1984: 169–92), Stephen J. Greenblatt notes the relish with which Guyon, guided by his accompanying Palmer, chastises the enchanting Acrasia and destroys her Bower of Bliss. Greenblatt summarises critical attitudes to the Bower of Bliss episode (Greenblatt 1984: 170–1), and then proceeds to distil the debate in his focus on the issue of the conflict between the moral rejection of everything this pleasure garden stands for, the extreme violence that the Bower provokes in Guyon, and the seductive power of the poetry through which the event is represented. He notes that:

> Temperance – the avoidance of extremes, the "sober government" of the body, the achievement of the Golden Mean – must be constituted paradoxically by a supreme act of destructive excess.
>
> (Greenblatt 1984: 172)

Extreme temptation is countered by excessive violence in a violent purgation that according to Greenblatt betrays a fascination with what has to be destroyed. Notwithstanding these critical qualms, the clean, sober (masculine) Protestantism that remains after the destruction in the figures of Guyon and his accompanying Palmer then proceeds to clean up after itself. The Palmer changes the various beasts in the garden back to their former human shapes and Acrasia is led off in captivity. This is the latest in a long line of luxurious feminine gardens that must be destroyed by the virtuous masculinity of the interloper. Spenser repeats the broad contours of the episode set in Amida's garden from Tasso's poem by means of a distilled representation of

Christian virtue, while the garden as a *topos* recalls an element of the romance tradition and before that an epic *motif* that stretches right back to Circe, via Rustam. Of course, the emblematic importance of this longstanding image reinforces its attractiveness as a *locus* of specifically Christian meanings.

The poem continues to make use of inherited techniques of this kind. Chastity appears in the form of the unconquerable woman Britomart, who is in love with the knight Artegal (the personification of Justice), although he does not initially know that she loves him, and she carries a lance that enables her to defeat any opponent in combat. The only time her weapons fail her is when she meets Artegal, and the allegorical point is made when he falls in love with her after defeating her in combat, indicating that it is appropriate for chastity to be chastely overcome by justice. Artegal initially fails in his own quest because he takes up the challenge of the Amazon warrior Radigund, who decrees that any man she defeats has to serve her in the clothing of a woman. In allegorical terms, Artegal loses because as a champion of justice he should never have agreed to her terms in the first place, but he is rescued when Britomart intervenes and kills her counterpart. The virtue of Courtesy is elaborated in the figure of Calidore, while Friendship in Book 4 is, fittingly, distributed across several constitutive figures. There are also various other major characters whose functions serve to link together the various parts of the overarching storyline.

This brief description does very little justice to the intricate complexities of the individual stories in Spenser's poem and their allegorical significance. Additionally, it should be remembered that the various constituent romance stories are ultimately contained, if somewhat uncomfortably, within this epic structure, and hence *The Faerie Queene* is positioned squarely within the ongoing literary history of the epic form as it emerges during this period. Clearly, the quest and the journey are epic *motifs* of longstanding provenance, but the relationships between them and the characters, and between the various characters themselves, owe more to the romance elements. Even though Spenser never managed anything like his intended composition, there are the beginnings of a story of a relationship leading to marriage between the questing Arthur and the Faerie Queene of the title, and the allegory therefore unites Arthur with Queen Elizabeth I in her Gloriana persona as part of a flattering gesture towards imperial British dominion. The ancient myth of an Arthur who supposedly ruled all of Britain is thus brought into the present through Spenser's poem.

The overall structure of *The Faerie Queene* therefore tries to subsume romance within epic, an impulse that is familiar from Tasso. If it fails, to recall David Quint's comments, it does so for very important reasons: in his Introduction to the *Orlando Furioso*, Guido Waldman blames Spenser's versification for this outcome, claiming that it is not English enough (in Ariosto 2008: xv). However, if there are much deeper currents of historical change operating upon the epic form, then it would seem sensible to look for more fundamental causes than these purely formal elements of the poem. Spenser offers something of a response to this criticism by addressing these issues in his letter to Raleigh (Spenser 1984: 15–18), entitled:

A LETTER OF THE AUTHORS EXPOUNDING HIS WHOLE INTENTION IN THE COURSE OF THIS WORKE: WHICH FOR THAT IT GIUETH GREAT LIGHT TO THE READER, FOR THE BETTER UNDERSTANDING IS HEREUNTO ANNEXED.

We may wonder why Spenser felt the need to include as part of the prefatory material for the poem a letter of explanation of his method and his intention along with the published poem. A clue emerges in the second half of the statement in the claim that the letter will enlighten the reader, enabling better understanding of what might on the surface seem obscure. There follows an address to Raleigh, and then the explanation itself that focuses on the problem of interpretation and the implied responsibilities of the reader:

Sir knowing how doubtfully all Allegories may be construed, and this booke of mine, which I have entituled the Faery Queene, being a continued Allegory, or darke conceit, I have thought good aswell for auoyding of gealous opinions and misconstructions, as also for your better light in reading therof.

(Spenser 1984: 15)

He goes on to explain that the poem aims to 'fashion' a gentleman, although there is a tension here between that purpose on the one hand, and the actual practice of reading on the other. Although Spenser is not an extreme Protestant, he is well aware that he has no direct authorial control over how his work will be understood and thus what meanings will be generated in the process of reading. The reason for this anxiety is located both in the unstable nature of allegory itself, which Spenser calls a "darke conceit", and in the fact that epic is no longer a communal phenomenon, whose interpretation extends beyond the purview of the individual reader. There is, it would appear, a danger inherent in Protestantism, where the individual (not the Church) is ultimately responsible for the production of meaning, even though regular instruction from the pulpit remained, and the institution of the Church was, under Elizabeth I, firmly under the control of the monarch. Notwithstanding this anxiety, Spenser then proceeds to elaborate a whole list of epic predecessors in support of his endeavour, from Homer right down to Tasso (Spenser 1984: 15).

Like Tasso at the outset of *The Liberation of Jerusalem*, Spenser thus has no clear conception of romance as generically distinct from epic as a narrative form: it simply comes later in a dynamic and vibrant tradition. This is important, because this uncertainty points to a much more complex literary historical context, in which, as we have seen, both genres interact with each other. It is perhaps this uncertainty about the distinction between the two forms that is part of the motivation for Spenser having to explain his own allegorical method. This does not, however, signal the death of epic, so much as an anxiety about the contemporary reception of the poem, and the registering of a contemporary sense of change in literary taste and political and cultural awareness.

THE LUSIADS

A consciousness of political and cultural change is not, however, unique to Protestant culture. The Portuguese poet Luis Vaz de

Camoes published his *Lusiads* in 1572, at the point at which Portuguese maritime endeavours were already beginning to be threatened by other powers. The importance of naval prowess led him to adopt the *Aeneid* as his direct model in a poem that has become the national epic of Portugal. The award-winning translator of Camoes' poem, Landeg White, touches on many of the issues raised above in relation to Spenser and his Italian models, as well as others pertinent to the Portuguese poem in and of itself. Camoes is not writing a romance in the style of his Italian contemporaries, so he does not look backwards nostalgically to an existence that has now been lost. Even so, there is still a sense of localised loss on the part of the poet, as White points out:

> In Camoes' single letter home from Goa, which he labels "the mother of villains and stepmother of honest men", there is already a strong sense of an empire in decline. French and English warships were already marauding and the Dutch were about to join the scene. The point is important, for underlying the manifest heroics of *The Lusiads* there is a note of elegy, of absences and regret. It had all happened before Camoes' time.
>
> (White in Camoes 2008: x)

Camoes' representation of the voyage of Vasco da Gama is tinged with the wistful yearning after a lost naval empire that, just like the romance form in its contemporary state, is in decline, but there is nevertheless an awareness that other rival seagoing empires are on the rise. *The Lusiads* embodies the excitement of an expanding worldview and at the same time it registers the transitory nature of the imperialist enterprise, at least in the Portuguese experience. This explains the retrospective casting of the prophecies made to da Gama towards the end of the poem regarding Portugal's future greatness, a greatness that is already passing at the point at which Camoes experiences its dominion at first hand:

> But in India, envy and ambition
> Boldly setting their faces against God

And all justice, will cause you–
No, not shame, no – but sorrow!

(Camoes 2008: 10.58 1–4)

As White suggests, Camoes' poem is situated at a moment of relative historical equilibrium and in a way *The Lusiads* is about to tilt towards the open seas away from the nostalgia of romance. Both romance and the new importance of the sea voyage are, of course, already catered for in the epic, as we saw in Chapter 1. But it is important to realise that at this historical juncture, the quest *motif* that has held sway for so long, and that had contained the epic form, is about to be replaced by the ancient marine voyage whose pedigree can be traced all the way back to the figures of Odysseus and, especially, Aeneas.

Many of the techniques utilised by Camoes are resolutely Virgilian, and much of the poem resonates with overtones of the *Aeneid*. Camoes could have taken the *Odyssey* as his model, and the fact that he does not do so can only be explained by the particular resonance of the *Aeneid* as a constitutive model for empire, which as we saw earlier, marks out its fundamental difference from Homer's poem. As White observes, *The Lusiads* is a literary symptom of the encounter between the classical past and the ever-expanding horizon of the Renaissance present: "[...] the constant weaving of his historical sources with the demands of the epic form and with personal thought and fresh observation are the very substance of *The Lusiads*" (in Camoes 2008: xii). White shows in some detail how this works (xii–xv), but he goes on to suggest that there is a further complication. The narrative is so relatively fresh in terms of the Renaissance European experience of overseas empire that it has not yet settled fully into an imperial pattern (xix–xx). This explains the disjointed nature of the representation of Islam and Muslim cultures, as well as those of other countries that the mariners either hear described, or that they encounter themselves (see, for example, White's description of stanzas 62–64 of canto V, at xii–xiii). Since the poem is a product of the peninsular experience, it may come as something of a surprise that it does not in fact adopt a crusading tone in the Spanish mould. However, Camoes is sensitive to major differences within Islam, and between Muslim states. Additionally, his newly expanding Christendom is not a monolith, as is shown by the ominous appearance in the poem of French ships as well as those of the Protestant English. At the same time, Islam is not reduced to one massive undifferentiated 'other' in the poem. This is entirely different from the representation of the Muslim adversaries of Roland in his various incarnations from *The Song of Roland* through to the Orlando figure of the late Italian romances.

Another difference between Camoes and his Italian and English contemporaries can be discerned in his use of allegory. The allegorical elements tend to appear when Camoes is making use of the classical deities. Even so, as White realises, they function as comic figures in the poem's development (in Camoes 2008: xvi). By reducing allegory to a series of comic effects, Camoes reduces the impact of its value as a mode of epic exposition. Whether or not this is intended is irrelevant, but what matters is that *The Lusiads* registers a movement away from the all-encompassing power of allegory. An excellent example occurs with the Isle of Love episode in the poem's last two cantos, in which Venus sets up a resting place for the weary voyagers. Unlike the Bower of Bliss in Spenser, or Amida's garden in Tasso, the sailors have no problems interacting with the inhabitants of Venus' island, with the result that there appears to be no need to represent allegorically any moral repugnance with the pleasures of the flesh. The example of *The Lusiads* shows that epic narratives remain capable of a wider variety than a purely allegorical exposition would imply, especially within the Virgilian tradition of the national epic trajectory.

MILTON

The Italianate and classical tradition culminates in England in Milton's *Paradise Lost* (Milton 1968). His poem is even more radically Protestant in its focus than Spenser's, and his affinities are with Du Bartas' Huguenot work *Première Semaine, ou Création du Monde* (1578). Milton does include allegory (notably the figures of Sin and Death at II.648ff and again at X.229–414), but in general he uses allegorical set-pieces sparingly, and as a committed Christian, his avowed purpose is to 'justify the ways of God to man' (I.26) and thereby to render the most seminal of all Christian narratives in the highest literary form. Like Dante, Milton uses the epic for an explicitly polemical religious purpose, and as a dedicated humanist, his debt to the classics is apparent in almost every line, as he replays in English verse the formal requirements so familiar from Virgil onwards. However, the pagan classical representation of the epic hero, together with the whole associated paraphernalia of multiple deities, is discarded in favour of a monotheistic Christian scheme. Milton depends upon the classical epic model, but he also transcends it, and this is exactly the same strategy that Virgil adopted in his appropriation of the Homeric model at the founding moment of imperial Rome.

It is no accident that it is the relation between the inherited classical tradition and the new Protestant recasting of it that has attracted most attention. Criticism seems divided along the Miltonic fault-line created by the conjunction of the pagan classics with the great Christian epic, and attention is most often focused on the debate around the extent to which Satan as the great antagonist attracts the sympathy of the reader, especially since he most closely fits the mould of the classical hero. Even though he is relegated to a secondary, instrumental position in the divine story, his structural importance all but accords him the status of the hero of the poem, as he attempts to reconstitute the 'human' in his own image. Milton would argue that Satan's apparent attractiveness is necessary because of the importance of free will in his *schema* and in Christianity as a religious doctrine where freedom of choice depends upon the attractiveness of evil. This attractiveness, however, is increased because he appears to be so much more active than his heavenly opposites. Indeed, the poem's insistence upon a demonic and subversive energy has proved attractive to subsequent generations, even though it is represented as perverse. The Romantic poet William Blake speaks for this tendency in his observation in *The Marriage of Heaven and Hell* that "Milton was of the devil's party without knowing it" (Blake 1983: 182). As a flawed epic hero he is made to confront the ineffable, which by definition and by comparison is beyond representation; David Quint, for example, goes so far as to label the war in heaven in Book VI as one that "verges on mock epic" (Quint 1993: 41). This is hardly surprising since even the most elevated of human languages is still post-lapsarian, and so by definition cannot represent divine perfection, something that Dante was acutely aware of at the end of the *Paradiso*. It has, however, laid Milton open to the often repeated criticism that he is temperamentally, at least, on the side of the fallen. Perhaps the most famous statement of this position is William Empson's book *Milton's God*, especially the chapter on the poem's depiction of God, who is characterised by Empson as remote and unsatisfying when compared with Satan's heroism (Empson 1981: 91–146).

However, there is another level of meaning in the poem that stands in more immediate relation to the historical and political context that informs Milton's writing more generally: the return to monarchical government and the failure of the Protestant English republic. Critics have noted how *Paradise Lost* stands in direct contrast to the Augustan propaganda of Restoration apologists by making God the final arbiter of all meaning (Quint 1993: 44–5). Quint, in particular, argues that since the deity has the power, the figure of Satan as adversary inevitably exemplifies the orientalising logic familiar from the imagery of Aeneas' shield; he argues that Satan's alternative (infernal) despotic power is a commentary on the figure of the returning Charles, even though that power was significantly reduced. For Quint, Milton's representation of Satan is part of an allegory that enables the disempowered Republican to continue to comment, albeit obliquely, on the contemporary politics of the period.

Milton's Satan is often seen as the inauguration of a new subjectivity, one that accords with an independent interiority. Whether or not this case is overstated, it marks an awareness that his poem looks forward to the rising age of individualism just as much as its classicism elaborates its debt to the past. Romantic poets such as Blake, whose sympathies pre-figure those of William Empson, could easily interpret Satan in accordance with their own romantic preconceptions that, as we have seen, included some sympathy for revolutionary energy. But there is also a further complication, since the figure of Milton marks the end of most literary histories of the epic. After him, the best that is achieved is the mock-heroic of Pope, followed by some scattered secondary works such as Southey's *Joan of Arc* (Southey 2005), and in the case of poets such as Wordsworth the trajectory of the epic is reduced to an exploration of the poet's own creative psyche in *The Prelude* (1805). It is almost as though the cult of the individual is in need of a grand initiatory gesture that can be made by a suitably powerful figure. Milton's epic achievement proves a serious threat to the future of the epic as it has evolved up to this point in history. This could explain why *Paradise Regained* (Milton 1990) seems inferior in comparison with the longer poem, even though its technical virtuosity is undoubted (but see Quint 1993: 325–7 for the shorter poem as political allegory). The same could be said by way of comparison about *Samson Agonistes* (also included in Milton 1990), a curious 'drama' that is often paired with *Paradise Regained* almost as a secondary epic, even though it is a formal tragedy. The romantic poets, especially Wordsworth and Coleridge, tried and failed to emulate Milton which, as we have seen in Chapter 1, the modern critic Harold Bloom represents an Oedipal struggle as an "anxiety of influence" in which the patriarch-poet is too strong to be supplanted.

THE EARLY NOVEL

If the pre-eminence of the figure of Milton obscures what is in fact a long-term historical development, then it would be appropriate to look for symptoms of the transformation of epic and allegory in other cultural forms. The early novel furnishes some examples that have striking similarities with the issues raised by the combination of romance and epic. The work of the fifteenth-century French monastic François Rabelais provides a whole host of demotic *grotesquerie* that is alien to the refined world of the aristocratic literary epic and its associated romance tradition (Rabelais 2006), while at the same time remaining dependent for its effects upon the traditional material of the epic.

Rabelais satirises many of the aristocratic values that informed both the romance and epic traditions. The one word which has come to sum up his technique and his achievement is the *carnivalesque*, a term that was coined by Mikhail Bakhtin in his book *Rabelais and His World* (Bakhtin 1984), and that represents an obverse anarchic prose alternative to the dominant epic and romance values and forms of his time. Bakhtin focuses on the language of the marketplace, as opposed to the discourses of epic and romance. He notes how the higher ideals of the traditional forms are undercut in Rabelais' *Gargantua and Pantagruel* by figures of excess. Instead, the emphasis is upon the decaying human body, which Bakhtin characterises by means of his conception of the "lower bodily stratum" and its constant regeneration in the energies of those who are oppressed. His work is consistently faithful to the overriding logic of the world he labels *carnivalesque*: the principle of comic inversion, as derived from the classical tradition of Menippean satire. It explains the importance of humour, undercutting elevated literary language of the kind that Western cultures have inherited from the epic, and he teased out the ways in which the grotesque imagery and logic of Rabelais' text combined into a genuinely populist art form, a kind of demotic prose epic.

The Rabelaisian outburst would seem to be at the opposite end of the spectrum from the *ethos* of what we might call the official epic or, indeed, the mock-epic. Even so, much of what he accomplished had a great deal in common with those elements in French popular culture that existed in the *Chansons de Geste*. As noted in Chapter 3, some of the Old French epic poems contain exactly the same kind of satirical inversions as Rabelais. These then reappear in the early novel form, after having been mostly excised both from the epic and from romance. The voyage for the Divine Bottle demonstrates some aspects of Rabelais' technique. There is a voyage, as in classical epic, but unlike that of Odysseus, for example, the aim of this quest is to find alcoholic beverage as opposed to leaving home on some exalted and exemplary pretext. The storyline therefore makes use of a well-known epic *motif* to diminish the impact of epic itself. It insinuates that the motivations ascribed to epic heroes may well be less exalted since Odysseus and his fellow heroes do initially leave Troy well laden with spoils, even though their war is idealised in comparison with the Rabelaisian search for purely bodily satisfaction. The reader does not need to know the *Odyssey* in detail in order to understand the trajectory of the narrative, but nevertheless the technique that Rabelais employs demands a degree of oscillation between two levels of knowledge simultaneously, in a manner that is analogous with the multiple strands prevalent in the popular drama of the Renaissance.

The reworking of epic elements that we have traced does not always, or necessarily, take the form of Rabelaisian prose, however. In England, Sir Philip Sidney condenses elements of romance and epic in a completely different way from Rabelais in *The Old Arcadia*, which he completed around 1580, and which we should differentiate from his later unfinished work, *The New Arcadia*. The earlier text is complete, and it represents an idealised pastoral world that seems to some extent to be under threat because of an ambiguous prophecy. The Arcadianism that results has its own pedigree within English literary history, but it is based on a convenient fiction: that Arcadia is a delightful location and that romantic events occur there. Sidney takes full advantage of his knowledge of the classical epic, combining it in a new prose form that, together with his awareness of the conventions of medieval and Renaissance romance, resembles the techniques of Spenser in *The Faerie Queene*.

The tone of Sidney's *Old Arcadia* is much lighter than the later version of it and, formally, it would be incorrect to call it a novel in the accepted sense of the term. The reason for this is the inclusion of poetic interludes (eclogues) that demonstrate Sidney's mastery of that form, and also the structure is derived from drama, with its five books corresponding to the five acts of a play. It is much more fruitful to conceive of *The Old Arcadia* as belonging to a new generic category, a freshly novel approach to literary fiction that does not accord with the old forms of epic, but which is as yet relatively unfixed, but that continues to utilise some recognisable elements of the earlier, more established form. The novelty of the form is reflected in the etymology of the word 'novel' and an emphasis on its relative newness in this period should help to avoid some of the baggage the term has accrued in its subsequent history. Readers who are used to later novels may not otherwise recognise this narrative as a novel at all.

Alan Sinfield locates Sidney's texts as the representation of a nexus of power relations in the Renaissance. He also describes how those relations are themselves worked by and through ideological interests and he goes on to analyse both text and context in an essay in his book *Faultlines: Cultural Materialism and the Politics of Dissident Reading*; for example, he analyses elements of Sidney's text as part of a larger reflection, in displaced form, of the politics of the court of Elizabeth I (Sinfield 1992: 93). However, embedded within Sidney's text is also an implied theory of narrative, since the epic tradition is full of displacements and representations that comprise sub-narratives available for reinterpretation in contemporary terms. Bearing this in mind, it is easy to see that Sidney not only borrows the material of romance for his novel text, but he also makes extensive use of epic components as well. Sinfield's account takes this fully into consideration as he moves from the specific historical positioning of the writer to a theorising of the prose fiction text in general. At the historical moment of its inception, the novel embodies conflicting possibilities, and as a dynamic, vibrant form, it provides a space within which particular kinds of political and cultural conflicts and anxieties are played out. Among the multiple influences to which this 'novel' kind of writing is exposed, are the narratives and techniques so familiar from the epic: journeys, exemplary representative aristocratic quests, and conflict.

The texts of Rabelais and Sidney offer examples of the different ways in which a number of aspects of the epic and romance are articulated and reworked in early prose fiction. Another early modern novelist, the Spanish writer Miguel de Cervantes, accomplished this amalgamation of techniques and *motifs* even more impressively, by means of the parody of the knightly quest. The narrative of *Don Quixote* systematically undoes chivalric romance; indeed, the translator of the Penguin edition, John Rutherford, notes how the book's structure replicates the episodic chance encounters familiar from the very narratives to which it refers (in Cervantes 2003: viii–ix), and the relatively open structure combines with a sense of experimentation to produce a text that is genuinely novel.

In a manner similar to Rabelais, Cervantes also utilises many of the demotic elements familiar from earlier epic tales such as the *Chansons de Geste*. In particular, the appearance of Sancho Panza after the start of the novel introduces the foil to the protagonist, which again harks back to the similar figures from the *Chansons de Geste*, such as Renewart in the *Song of William*. Similarly, the allegorical figure of the Dwarf who accompanies Redcrosse Knight in Book 1 of *The Faerie Queene* is one of many 'varlets' who accompany the various protagonists of Spenser's poem on their respective quests, adding another layer to the parody of epic that is so famous for its depiction of the ageing knight tilting at windmills. It is the relationship between Sancho Panza and the strange adventurer Don Quixote that underpins the development of the rest of Cervantes' novel. This relationship personifies a fundamental dialogism into the novel form at its very outset, in which a dominant narrative voice is juxtaposed against another, more demotic alternative that challenges its authority. The term 'dialogism' is taken from Mikhail Bakhtin's influential analysis of the novel as a literary form, *The Dialogic Imagination* (Bakhtin 1975). Here he argues that the narrative of the novel as a genre is not 'monologic' – the product of a single authorial voice – but a tissue of interpolated voices that he identifies through his use of the term 'heteroglossia'. The result is a generic openness that, Bakhtin argues, appears most often in the form of internal textual relations between characters, as exemplified in the various forms of narrative exposition that the writer deploys.

The Bakhtinian model sheds a great deal of light on the complex text of *Don Quixote* and on some aspects of the text's composition and reception. Like Rabelais, Cervantes wrote in intermittent bursts; indeed Part 2 is the result of another writer trying to pirate the characters. Cervantes takes advantage of this situation not only to continue where he left off at the end of Part 1, but also to incorporate his rival into the story. The rival is then misplaced in turn, and this simply extends to another level the dialogism that already exists in Part 1, between the author figure and various narrative personae. As with Sidney, the use of sub-narratives throughout echoes the epic, but in *Don Quixote* the various narrative levels work in very specific ways. The insistence on their use and the various relationships between them and what is presumably Cervantes' (provisional) authorial voice, marks this novel as a radical exploration of writing and representation. As well as being about the Don and his servant, it is also 'about' writing. The first novels are self-consciously aware of their status as literary artefacts, often using humour to puncture the seriousness of the knightly quest. In this respect, they have a great deal in common with some aspects of the popular stage. Francis Beaumont's play *The Knight of the Burning Pestle* (c. 1612) echoes Cervantes and others as they find their way into the English prose and drama of the period. As Andrew Gurr points out in the Critical Introduction to his edition of the play, satirical content is rendered by means of sub-narratives that replay in English many of the concerns and techniques of Cervantes' novel (in Beaumont 1968, 2–5).

Elements familiar from the epic continue to be important for the novel as it develops. Aphra Behn's *Oroonoko* (1688) replicates at a formal level the epic introductory verses common in the Virgilian tradition:

> I do not pretend, in giving you the history of this royal slave, to entertain my reader with the adventures of a feigned hero whose life and fortunes fancy may manage at the poet's pleasure.
>
> (Behn 2003: 9)

Virgil had used the first person in his narrative, but he did not address the assumed reader with such direct familiarity. Behn proposes to tell the story of a royal hero in adversity, but not in the overly imaginative ways of epic poetry. Epic is available to Behn as part of a process of colonising the form, not for direct imitation, and she uses it selectively in a new form that is more in keeping with the emerging sensibilities of the culture of the individual and its emphasis on the inner psychology of characters and their ability to generate reader sympathy (Janet Todd in Behn 2003: xv–xvi). The emotional engagement of the reader in the lives of fictional characters will become one of the most important features of the rise of the novel as it develops across the next two centuries.

The case of Behn demonstrates how epic was being used by a rising social class and in a form that could be more easily accessible to rising numbers of readers. This process continues into the next century, and Ian Watt notes in this context the importance of literary demographics at the beginning of the eighteenth century:

> Many eighteenth-century observers thought that their age was one of remarkable and increasing popular interest in reading. On the other hand, it is probable that although the reading public was large by comparison with previous periods, it was still very far from the mass reading public of today.
>
> (Watt 1963: 36).

This historical moment produces a relatively small and highly literate reading public and Watt goes on to relate the epic to the English culture of the eighteenth century in his chapter on Fielding, whose novels he describes as "the comic epic in prose" (Watt 1963: 249). Watt's formulation suggests that Fielding's novels develop in prose an equivalent to the mannered mock-heroic epic style of Pope. The narrative strategies and *motifs* of the epic are by this time in the process of becoming subsumed into the new world of the novel, as well as being utilised in poetry for mock heroic purposes; in sociological terms both developments accompany the rise of the individual reader.

5

EPIC IN THE AGE OF
THE INDIVIDUAL

Epic poems continue to be produced after Milton, as part of the overall ongoing poetic engagement with the classics. However, by the early nineteenth century, epic seems to lose something of its cultural centrality, even though it continues to be regarded as the highest poetic form. A good example is the *Columbiad* of the American poet Joel Barlow, first published in 1807, an enlarged version of a previous poem entitled *The Vision of Columbus*, neither of which was especially successful. David Quint places the *Columbiad* in its historical context towards the end of a discussion of European overseas expansionism, noting the difficulty of epic production in the changed circumstances of the early nineteenth century:

> In an age of reason and science, Barlow is unsure whether the mythical creations of poetry retain any persuasive power – no one believes in giants any more – and he goes on (331–94) to make the case against slavery on the grounds of rational self-interest. Yet, he holds out the hope that the epic figure of Atlas and his chilling

prophecy may still rouse his countrymen to emotional sympathy. Both Barlow and Camoes, anxious about the continuity of a kind of classical epic awe in a modern era increasingly sceptical toward poetic fictions, vest that awe in personifications of the victimized [...]

(Quint 1993: 129–30)

Barlow uses epic as part of an argument against the institution of slavery, but as Quint realises, the American poet is at best hesitant in his project. Barlow shares with Camoes an underlying recognition that the force of epic can no longer be taken for granted. In the wake of the eighteenth-century Enlightenment emphasis on science and reason and the scepticism generated by an increasingly scientific worldview, the form commanded less widespread attention than it had done previously. As we saw in the previous chapter, epic *motifs* migrated to the emerging novel form, while some of its characteristic tropes and its elevated tone were to become parodied in the novels of Henry Fielding and the poetry of Alexander Pope as mock-heroic.

POETRY

Knowledge of the classics remains an essential marker of a full education well into the eighteenth century, even if many writers shy away from producing their own epic work; indeed, a poet such as Alexander Pope can even practise his craft against epic, and also against courtly society. As a translator of Homer and Statius, Pope was well versed in the classical tradition, especially in the epic, although he did not write serious epic poetry himself, choosing instead to follow a tradition of parodying the heroic epic that had begun in English with Samuel Butler's *Hudibras* (the first full publication of which was in 1684) and John Dryden's *Mac Flecknoe* (written around 1678, and first published in 1682). These poems appropriated the comic inversion of romance and epic from novels such as *Don Quixote* and rendered it in a poetry that applied the elevated form of epic to trivia, as an instrument of excoriating criticism. Pope used the technique in *The Dunciad* (published in several versions, the final one in 1743) as well as in *The Rape of the Lock* (published in its final form in 1717), which is usually considered to be the finest example of the genre. Comprising five cantos, *The Rape of the Lock* is an impressive demonstration of learning turned against the epic by the application of a high style to the most inconsequential of occurrences. All of the standard generic elements are rehearsed, such as the initial invocation to the muse (I.1–6); references to "equipage" as armaments (I.45 and I.100); spirits whose pedigree can be traced back to *Paradise Lost* (I.69–70); foretelling and fate (I.109); altars and sacrifice (I.121ff and II.35ff); and warfare (game of cards at III.25ff). There is also an extended parody of allegory (IV.11ff). The elevated style, vocabulary and structure are all derived from epic and are used to ridicule the occasion of the poem, the 'rape' of Belinda by the cutting of a lock of her hair, and as a means of providing an excoriating critique of the social life of the heroine. The social satirical element so common in Pope works through these means to attack every aspect of courtly behaviour; the following reference to Queen Anne offers a good example of Pope's method:

> Here thou, great ANNA! whom three realms obey,
> Dost sometimes counsel take – and sometimes Tea.

(III.7–8)

The movement from affairs of state to a cup of tea neatly encapsulates the poem's whole endeavour, inaugurating a technique that T.S. Eliot's early twentieth-century poem *Prufrock*, which also deploys elements of mock epic, will later utilise.

The knowing abuse of epic is so structurally central to Pope's poem that if it were not for its subject matter it would be a superb example of a short epic in its own right. Pope is aware that his sophisticated reading public will delight in teasing out every possible allusion and stylistic twist, and this marks his poem out as being different from the novels that lead to the emergence of the mock epic. For Cervantes and Rabelais, a multiplicity of meanings can be generated by their anti-epic narratives. With Pope, however, knowledge of the form is so embedded in his poem that it is central to his project, and the mockery requires prior knowledge on the part of the reader of a very specific kind. Having said this, the complex uses of epic in the poem provide the modern reader with an excellent way to learn the basic elements of epic poetic form and techniques.

Towards the end of the eighteenth century, the coming of the French Revolution elicited enthusiastic reactions from English writers even if some of them, such as Coleridge and Wordsworth, subsequently abandoned their initial Republican impulses. This was the immediate political context for the emergence of Romanticism, a complex phenomenon that provided the focus for a number of social, political and cultural movements. Part of the Romantic sensibility was a reaction against the tastes of the Enlightenment, replacing the guiding light of classical reason with the primacy of emotional response and in particular emphasising the cognitive and creative role of the imagination. In English poetry the result was not so much a disengagement from, or an abandonment of, classical epic but a refocusing of the poetic relationship with it. For example, Southey's epic poem about the medieval French heroine *Joan of Arc* (1796) does not end with Joan's death at the hands of her English adversaries, but with the successful re-imposition of French power. However, Joan's death is foretold in a manner that is exactly modelled on Homer's treatment of the figure of Achilles in *The Iliad*.

As already noted in Chapter 4, the status of Milton was especially troubling for the Romantics, generating an "anxiety of influence", to use Harold Bloom's term. The revolutionary poet Blake celebrated the figure of Milton as epic forebear because of his use of the Bible, comparing Milton's accomplishment with the classics in his preface to *Milton* (Blake 1983: 513). However, poets such as Wordsworth and Coleridge found it impossible to produce successful epics after Milton, and this tendency continued through the nineteenth century, in spite of the revival of medievalism in the writings of poets such as Tennyson. In *The Prelude,* Wordsworth refashioned epic by replacing heroic action with an account of the growth of the poet's imagination, thus placing primary emphasis on the importance of the individual creative consciousness. Significantly, the work remained unfinished. Keats added the phrase *A Poetic Romance* as a subtitle to his poem *Endymion*, but he also felt the need to supplement it with a further description: "*The stretched metre of an antique song*" (Keats 1983: 105). He employed a similar tactic in relation to *Hyperion: A Fragment* (Keats 1983: 283–307) and *The Fall of Hyperion: A Dream* (435–49), both of which, like *The Prelude,* are incomplete. Shelley's *Alastor* used allegory to frame his conception of the imagination (Shelley 2009: 92–111), and in his preface to *Laon and Cythna* he specifically noted that it is "IN THE STANZA OF SPENSER" (Shelley 2009: 130), aligning his poem with both the stanza form and the allegorical style of the earlier poet. Byron's *Don Juan* begins polemically with a dedication that challenges the older generation of Romantic poets (Southey and Wordsworth), effectively accusing them of selling out (Byron 1991: 373–7). Yet another unfinished work, it is a long romance that uses all the techniques of the form to chronicle the wandering adventures of its hero, most of which are anything but heroic. In this respect Byron echoes the mock epics of Pope, but his focus is resolutely on the transgressive individual, and on the particular experience that is very dear to this particular poet.

The Romantics were therefore well aware of the possibilities afforded by epic, but they also felt constrained by it. In his abridged version of Coleridge's *Notebooks*, Seamus Perry includes a section in which Coleridge produces a critical appraisal of *Paradise Lost:* "The Serpent by which the ancients emblem'd the Inventive faculty appears to me in its mode of motion most exactly to emblem a writer of Genius" (Coleridge 2002: 17). The serpent's sinuous movement in the Garden of Eden symbolised for Coleridge the creative impulse of a great "Genius", one which he capitalises because of the primacy he places on the individual. At the same time, however, Coleridge's celebration of the Miltonic epic achievement is extremely deferential, constructing a Milton who is so elevated that it is difficult to emulate him, and impossible to outdo him.

Wordsworth shared Coleridge's ambivalence when it came to epic, conflating its deities with the Kantian sublime by means of epic, while at the same time insisting on the primary importance of the poet himself as the mediator of an experience capable of transcending human comprehension. A particularly condensed version of many of these concerns can be found in the following passage from *The Prelude:*

> I dipped my oars into the silent lake,
> And, as I rose upon the stroke, my boat
> Went heaving through the water like a swan;
> When from behind that craggy steep till then
> The horizon's bound, a huge peak, black and huge,
> As if with voluntary power instinct
> Upreared its head. I struck and struck again,
> And growing still in stature the grim shape
> Towered up between me and the stars, and still,
> For so it seemed, with purpose of its own
> And measured motion like a living thing,
> Strode after me.

(l. 374–85)

In this extract, nature is endowed with a terrifying superhuman force that is intent on pursuing the fearful poet, whose humanity is sketched against the scale of its epic power. *The Prelude* epitomises the Romantic relationship with epic in several ways. First of all, it is Part One of a grand career-spanning autobiographical epic that was planned by Wordsworth, but as with some of the other examples we have seen, was never finished (*The Excursion* is Part Two). Secondly, it demonstrates an awareness of some kind of power beyond the human, a sublime presence that can be glimpsed only through poetic inspiration, but not easily described or defined. Thirdly, since this episode occurred when Wordsworth was still a schoolboy, it denotes the moment of the awakening of his poetic calling, which he elaborates over the next 20 or so lines of the poem. Fourthly, and crucially, it is about *him*: the poet is the hero of his own epic, and the call of his imagination will be his epic journey. This final point signifies a major transformation for epic writing as the form moves away from its engagement with national identity to a Romantic conception of personal poetic identity.

The Romantic emphasis on the individual imagination is, however, not the only major long-term transformation that epic undergoes during this period. Wordsworth and Coleridge begin by welcoming the French Revolution, but end up opposing the excesses of the Jacobin terror. Their changing position points to some form of alienation from the emerging modern nation-state, even though the English Romantics go on to furnish it with several Poet Laureates. However, this does not necessarily cause a split between works that represent national identity on the one hand, and those that focus on the individual on the other. The two often go together, as in the career of the exiled Polish Romantic poet Mickiewicz, who wrote the Polish national epic *Pan Tadeusz* in exile from his homeland.

A variation does emerge in the relationship between epic and nationalism during this period, with the retrospective construction of a pseudo-national epic history becoming a peculiar feature of the Romantic landscape. A particularly well-known instance can be found in the works of Ossian, first published in a collected edition in 1765 that includes an epic poem about the life of the Hero Fingal:

> James Macpherson claimed that Ossian was based on an ancient Gaelic manuscript. There was just one problem. The existence of this manuscript was never established.
>
> (Macpherson 2007: vii)

If epic was so difficult to write in this period, why did writers construct epics at all, especially by inventing texts like that of Ossian that purport to rework earlier narratives? There are two possible answers to this question, each of which reveals only part of the story. The first is that epic still retains its cultural status, even if it proves impossible to write. The second is that for some writers national identity was an issue, especially if we consider the enforced marginalisation of Gaelic cultures during the nineteenth century, a situation that was paralleled by the partition of Poland between Prussia, Austria-Hungary and Russia. It can also be found in Wales, with the reinstitution of a regular cultural festival, the Eisteddfod, from 1789 onwards (which is, not coincidentally, the same year as the French Revolution) and the first publication of a version of the *Mabinogion* in 1795.

Epic provided an appropriate literary register in which poets from supposedly subjugated cultures could articulate their concerns, especially when resurrecting or indeed constructing a mythic past.

There is another invented work of epic that parallels *Ossian*, showing that the impetus behind such productions was not limited to Scotland or Wales. In Finland, which had been subsumed into the Russian Empire as a Grand Duchy, the creation of a national epic known as the *Kalevala* emerged from a situation parallel to that of Scotland, which had become part of the United Kingdom after the Act of Union of 1707. However, in the Finnish case the epic is retrospectively produced out of a disparate set of folk tales which the editor, Lonnrot, strung together into a loose narrative structure. In this sense his work departs significantly from that of Macpherson. Keith Bosley writes:

> From a Western point of view the *Kalevala* is a double anachronism, an epic produced at a time when epic was regarded as a thing of the past, set in a world more archaic than that of *Beowulf*.
>
> (Bosley in Lonnrot 2008: xiv)

Epic may well have been regarded as a thing of the past, but its cultural status made it a powerful tool for those who wanted to assert national identity by seeking to re-create a national history; indeed, as Bosley notes that despite the difficulties Romantic poets encountered when trying to write epic, "epic had a new lease of life thanks to Romanticism" (in Lonnrot 2008: xiv). First published in 1835, the *Kalevala* appeared a generation after the German, French and English Romantics. The translation theorist Andre Lefevere argues in an essay on the *Kalevala* that the conceptual framework in which Lonnrot placed the Finnish tales already existed before he began his project: the epic (Lefevere 1998), and that he did so precisely because epic still possessed an exalted cultural status.

EPIC AND THE NOVEL

Even if David Quint is right about the inability of poets to produce new epic forms, the influence of epic nevertheless affects other genres. This has already been seen with the early novel, which continues to develop partly by incorporating epic *motifs* and narrative techniques into its structures. The *picaresque* novels of the eighteenth century provide many examples, although of course their main characters are not of recognisably heroic stature. In this respect the rogues, adulterers and other disreputable characters trace a double line of descent from the epic as classically conceived, but also from Rabelais and Cervantes as the progenitors of mock epic. Eponymous novels such as Defoe's *Moll Flanders*, Fielding's *Tom Jones* and Sterne's *Tristram Shandy* offer the most obvious examples since they extend the tradition of lively burlesque without abandoning their connection with epic altogether.

Epic elements are incorporated into the eighteenth-century novel through the device of the *picaresque,* especially the *motif* of the journey as it occurs in *Gulliver's Travels* and again in Sterne's *A Sentimental Journey*. In Fielding's novels *Tom Jones* and *Joseph Andrews* epic heroism is 'democratised' in so far as the heroes are either foundlings or minor figures in the community to whom unfortunate things happen. The sheer vitality of most of these fictions drives the novel form to a point where it takes over some of the functions that previously belonged to epic. Similar points can be made in relation to the supernatural elements that appear in many novels, especially in Gothic fiction. Mary Shelley's early nineteenth-century novel *Frankenstein* is a particularly good example, because of the way it amalgamates science and religion, aligning them with a long narrative tradition that can be traced back to Miltonic epic. Indeed, Shelley's text explores the intertextual relationships between all of these elements in an effort to raise the question of the status of Frankenstein as an epic hero who, like Renaissance heroes such as Marlowe's Faustus or Milton's Satan, over-reach themselves by usurping divine power. In some respects Shelley mounts a critique of the *masculine* epic hero whose behaviour in accordance with the claims of science is shown to backfire disastrously. In such a context, it makes sense to try to theorise the relationship between the epic, the spread of print culture and the rise to prominence of the novel. With the spread of literacy, the growth of a middle class and the subsequent relative democratising of the act of reading, historical forms such as the epic are assimilated into new forms of understanding. The emerging cultural, social and economic structures absorb the scope of the epic, while the concept of what we might call the exemplary or representative life is revised.

There is a further consequence of this long-term literary shift that impinges upon the epic itself. Epic poetry retains a residual status, but in a relatively circumscribed way, although some of its elements remain dynamic and are amenable to adaptation in a variety of ways. As this movement accelerates, so eventually the epic is emptied of its prior associations, with the result that as a form it can be appropriated for a variety of purposes. This is one of the reasons why David Quint can argue that the epic fails after the Renaissance, although its failure is not a catastrophe in itself so much as an indication of the novel's appropriation of its distinctive tropes. Thus it is possible to relate the decline in the affective power of epic to a corresponding rise of other literary forms.

A historical and theoretical account of epic as it evolves during the eighteenth century needs to take into account the importance of individualism. Epic and the novel both constitute sites in which different forms of communality and individualism are played out and contested. The Romantic poets sought to enhance the power of the individual artistic imagination, at the same time as the novel attempted to represent the individual life in its full social and domestic existence. However, the novel not only makes use of narratives descended from epic, it also enhances and refines them to the point where the form itself eventually attains a cultural status that is at least equal to the residual aura enjoyed by the epic, as it becomes the most socially pervasive of all powerful literary forms. In his influential account of the rise of the historical novel, the Hungarian Marxist critic Georg Lukacs argued that the narrative form that mediated between historical drama and the epic was the historical novel, the vehicle *par excellence* of bourgeois ideology as it reflected the epic rise of the middle class to literary pre-eminence (Lukacs 1983: 89–105). According to Jerome de Groot, Lukacs claimed that the novels of Sir Walter Scott indicate the historical juncture at which this bourgeois culture engaged with its own history in its rise to prominence:

> Essentially, then, the uproar of the times led to a new sense of historicity, manifest in the notion of historical progress, the possibility of change, and the individuated importance of these concepts. Specifically, these changes were expressed through the historical form of that genre.
>
> (de Groot 2010: 26)

Previously, an engagement with such concepts was the carefully circumscribed role of the epic, where the hero was an exemplary representative of a social order, which recalls our discussion of Aristotle in Chapter 2. However, in a society in which one very large social class rises to prominence, the epic requires to be adapted in such a way as to emphasise the emergence of 'novel' social forces that require their own distinct narratives. In this way, the focus on an emerging literary form was calculated to produce a supposedly more 'realistic' representation of experience. It is this that allows for a distance to be created between the adoption of a mock heroic style and 'real life' where there is a gap (as in Pope and Fielding) between the style of representation and a much more tawdry 'reality'. The realist novel arises when the narrative focuses on the quotidian private lives and psychological motives of ordinary individuals as distinct from the community, as a consequence of the growing distinction between private and public spheres. In this way the novel becomes more documentary and descriptive, and accordingly the 'epic' elements begin to drain away except that in so far as they function as a marker of cultural and social status they are retained by a social class that uses them to validate its power and position. Fielding used his mockery of the pretensions of epic to prick the delusions of an upper class that deluded itself into thinking that it lived life at the level of epic, and after him the 'epic' novel becomes more and more the form that speaks for a rising class, rather than being deployed as an instrument of ridicule.

The novel continues through this literary and historical process into movements such as Modernism, and with multiple variations. Peter Childs offers an account of the internal discussion among novelists about the novel form in his book *Modernism* (Childs 2008: 80–90), where he describes how Modernist writers self-consciously reacted against their realist predecessors, especially in terms of technique. Many of these writers used classical allusion, but the movement with which they became associated went one step further. According to Childs, for example, it is possible to read James Joyce's Modernist novel *Ulysses* (published in its entirety 1922, the same year as T.S. Eliot's poem *The Waste Land*) without knowing a great deal about its deployment of episodes from Homer's *Odyssey* (Childs 2008: 214–16). As we saw earlier, this is reminiscent of possible responses to romance and epic such as those that appeared in the writings of Rabelais and Cervantes, although the way these *motifs* are managed in the earlier texts partially obscures a powerful initiatory moment in prose writing. Joyce, however, extends this practice in such a way that a full appreciation of his novel (as indeed with Rabelais and Cervantes) depends upon a whole series of intertextual encounters with Homer, as can be seen in the following example from *Ulysses:*

> The three girl friends were seated on the rocks, enjoying the evening scene and the air which was fresh but not too chilly. Many a time and oft were they wont to come there to that favourite nook to have a cosy chat beside the sparkling waves and discuss matters feminine.

(Joyce 1985: 344)

What seems at first sight to be an innocuous evening scene observed by Leopold Bloom, the Ulysses figure in the novel, is directly analogous to Odysseus' encounter with Nausicaa in Book VI of the *Odyssey*.

There are therefore two structuring layers in *Ulysses*, one contemporary and modern, the other ancient and classical. The interplay between the two does not necessarily give more importance overall to either, but it does add to the book's sense of dynamism. It also relates Homer's epic to the Modernist text without privileging the traditional discourse of the epic. In this *schema* the novel is no longer simply indebted to the epic, it appropriates it. Epic status now belongs to the novel and in this respect it does make sense to talk about epic novels.

FROM MODERNISM TO POST-MODERNISM

The Modernist novel continues to move further away from epic poetry, especially after the Great War, and so too does Modernist poetry, T.S. Eliot's *The Waste Land* providing an epitaph; a free-form composition, it is a plea for order in the face of the cataclysmic disorder exemplified by its repetition of half-digested cultural references, many of them derived from epic. The poem longs for a return to an organic culture in which the epic hero is once more a representative figure, and for Eliot all that remains of this culture after the cataclysm is fragments, and so we may say that the poem invokes epic by its absence. Elsewhere, in poems such as *The Love Song of J. Alfred Prufrock*, Eliot reduces epic heroism to the level of trivial postures:

And indeed there will be time
To wonder 'Do I dare?' and, 'Do I dare?'
Time to turn back and descend the stair,
With a bald spot in the middle of my hair.

(Eliot 1974: 4)

Daring action here turns into a decision whether or not to go down a flight of stairs, and elsewhere Prufrock rejects the possibility of identifying with Hamlet as an heroic figure.

Eliot's poems certainly show epic in what appears to be its death throes in one part of Europe, but it is still possible to detect a relatively positive engagement with epic elsewhere. Greek culture has retained a much greater sense of its epic history than many others, but when Nikos Kazantzakis wrote his sequel to *The Odyssey* after World War II, he occasioned a great deal of literary turmoil. The debate is described by Kimon Friar in the introduction to his English translation (Kazantzakis 1958: ix–x), where he explicitly compares the response to Kazantzakis' poem with the critical reception of Joyce's *Ulysses*, unhesitatingly referring to Joyce's novel as an epic (in Kazantzakis 1958: x). In the case of Kazantzakis, the symbolism engendered by the hero's wanderings is carefully constructed and underpins the philosophical material of his poem (xii–xxiv). The experience of modernity makes it virtually impossible to integrate epic considerations of the divine into the narrative, since it is the effects of the exterior world upon the interiority of the individual subject that take precedence. What matters much more to Kazantzakis is the importance of individual experience, a feature that Alberto Manguel also draws attention to in his description of the failure rather than the success of the hero:

> He is a king, a soldier, a lover, the unhappy founder of a utopian community in Africa, but he is never successful in his enterprises. And yet, for this Ulysses, failure is less important than experience.
>
> (Manguel 2007: 201)

Kazantzakis does not simply replicate Homer's *Odyssey,* nor does he even privilege it as a canonical text that is part of a founding moment for a new historical epoch. Rather, for him epic is not something ossified, but dynamic, and both he and Joyce seem much more enthusiastic in their Modernist appropriations of epic than, say, T.S. Eliot; certainly, neither could be accused of treating their source material with any great solemnity.

Another renovation of epic, this time in the field of Drama, is attempted by Bertolt Brecht in Germany. His revolutionary epic theatre seeks to reinvigorate what had become a tired bourgeois theatre by reinventing it. He is not alone; in his Preface to *Miss Julie* (1888), August Strindberg explains the rationale behind his reinvention of tragic drama: "For the problem of social ascent or decline, of higher or lower, better or worse, man or woman, is, has been and will be of permanent interest" (Strindberg 1964: 100). Strindberg removed the classical deities from drama, and reconstituted the 'hero' figure as a combination of both 'psychological' and external forces. Brecht, however, who was far less committed to the 'naturalism' of his predecessor, placed far more emphasis on how the individual was *produced* by social and historical forces, in an effort to dissuade his audiences from identifying with 'characters' onstage. This was part of a much wider critique of the affective power of Aristotelian drama. He designed his own drama so as to lay open to the full view of the audience the mechanisms of representation. Indeed, he uses the term 'epic' in the same way that Lukacs thinks of the novel as a representation of those forces that constitute a 'society' and that shape the individual, whatever their historical epic status. One of his fullest statements comes in the form of notes to an opera (Brecht 1978: 33–42). Especially important is a *schema* by which he compares dramatic theatre with epic theatre, where the column for dramatic theatre is headed "plot", while for epic theatre, the equivalent is "narrative" (see Table 5.1).

Table 5.1

DRAMATIC THEATRE	EPIC THEATRE
plot	narrative
implicates the spectator in a stage situation	turns the spectator into an observer, but
wears down his capacity for action	arouses his capacity for action
provides him with sensations	forces him to take decisions
experience	picture of the world
the spectator is involved in something	he is made to face something
suggestion	argument
instinctive feelings are preserved	brought to the point of recognition
the spectator is in the thick of it, shares the experience	the spectator stands outside, studies
the human being is taken for granted	the human being is the object of the enquiry
he is unalterable	he is alterable and able to alter
eyes on the finish	eyes on the course
one scene makes another	each scene for itself
growth	montage
linear development	in curves
evolutionary determinism	jumps
man as a fixed point	man as a process
thought determines being	social being determines thought
feeling	reason

Brecht's alternatives to what he considered the 'traditional' Aristotelian theatre constituted a revolution both in structure and content, forming the basis for the operation of his 'alienation effect' (*Verfremdungseffekt*). His *schema* employs the time-honoured method of the inversion principle, and the fundamental objective of this technique is to disrupt the identification of the audience with the action, radically undermining their sympathetic engagement with what is presented. Brecht's audience is required to be dynamic, not passive, and is encouraged not to be absorbed into the dramatic action, but to analyse what is represented on the stage as a full dramatisation of those forces that determine how individuals and society work. As part of this process he consciously appropriates the term 'epic', as a means of returning it to its more communal inclusive roots in an attempt to rescue it from its bourgeois association with the private domestic sphere and with elitist art.

It can of course be questioned just how successful Brecht was in his project. The play that is most often described as the epitome of his drama, *Mother Courage and Her Children*, attempts to show how war and capitalism brutalise its characters, especially Mother Courage herself. And yet it cannot be guaranteed that a play-going audience will in fact react in the way Brecht envisaged, indeed it is possible to perceive Mother Courage's heroism as having its source in her resilient 'character', rather than being produced by the war she follows. This would be to domesticate her for a bourgeois perspective, transforming her into an autonomous 'individual' as opposed to analysing her as a focus of social and political contradictions to which she is herself subjected. The same argument might be advanced in relation to Brecht's complex play *Galileo*, where the contradictions are even more perplexing, providing even more potential for recuperating the action for a bourgeois perspective. This proviso notwithstanding, Brecht's deployment of the term 'epic' for his theatre provides an indication of the fact that, as we have already seen in poetry and the novel, epic and its narratives continued to exert a powerful influence on the literary and dramatic imagination even after the carnage of the First World War. Indeed, this was to be the case in the burgeoning culture of film that deployed epic *motifs* in new and innovative ways such as 'Expressionism', especially after the Second World War, when epic and biblical narratives were revived as part of the process of reaffirming national and religious identities.

Brecht's dramatisation of the social contradictions that he attributed to the operations of capitalism, harmonised with some of the formal, although not political, properties of Modernism. His location of a 'popular' voice bears comparison with other hitherto subjugated voices that were beginning to be heard in the twentieth century. Nowhere was this more in evidence than in the colonies of the British Empire, in a growing awareness of the politics of colonialism. Attempts were beginning to be made to wrest 'literature' and its various forms away from those who had come to regard them as instruments of colonial authority and legitimacy, and to invest them with alternative and subversive meanings. Joyce's *Ulysses* was the work of an expatriate Irishman living in Paris, and it deployed the *topoi* of the classical epic from what was, and continues to be, a politically troubled geographical location, a divided Ireland.

A later example of just such a reworking emerges with the Caribbean poet Derek Walcott, whose poem *Omeros* (1990) demonstrates conclusively that far from being dead, the epic is alive, vibrant and capable of registering the concerns of those who had been the subjects of empire. Walcott's text engages with those imperial epic antecedents from the perspective of post-colonialism, where the representations of culture inevitably confront the mechanisms and the effects of imperial power. In his poem, Walcott also engages explicitly with the relationship between the epic and gender by making it clear that it is the figure of Helen who occasions the events of Homer's poems, although the Greek narratives are mostly concerned with the deeds of masculine heroes. In contrast with the Homeric archetype, the 'ravished' Helen is of central symbolic importance in Walcott's poem, so much so that she is often identified with the island of St Lucia itself:

> [...] the island was once
> named Helen, its Homeric association

rose like smoke from a siege; the Battle of the Saints
was launched with that sound.

(Walcott 1990: 31)

This is an extraordinarily precise rendering of one of the central
features of imperialist ideology: the unexplored land figured as
female that has prevailed from the sixteenth century, right down
to Conrad's fictional account of colonisation, *Heart of Darkness*
(first published in serial form in 1899). In this passage, Walcott
explicitly links this figure with a paradisal origin, together with
the history of imperial warfare and the Western cultural tradition.

Robert D. Hamner has produced a detailed analysis of Walcott's poem in his book entitled *Epic of the Dispossessed* (Hamner
1997), which suggestively calls to mind the Brechtian revolution
in epic theatre. His chapter divisions imply a framing narrative:
first section, "Walcott's Odyssey", final section "Home From the
Sea", but within the structure is another internal frame: second
section "Philoctete's Wound", penultimate section "The Healing".
Sandwiched in between these two structures are "The Battle over
Helen" and three travel passages (to Africa, North America and
Europe). The form here obviously owes a great deal to Homer's
Odyssey, but the individual books that make up the poem as a
whole possess an internal dynamism that pulls strongly against the
Homeric framework to produce a sense of constant movement, like
the rhythms of the sea. Hamner's title makes explicit the link
between epic and the processes of imperial dispossession, emphasising that Walcott's poem allows the dispossessed to speak.

What in Brecht was an issue of 'social class' becomes in
Walcott a question of national and cultural identity, where colonialism is of such epic scope that it can be shown to affect a
whole culture. The noise and visibility of contemporary culture
should not obscure the fact that, in some parts of the world at
least, epic is very much still alive and the work of writers such
as Walcott continues to inherit verbal epic traditions that survive,
albeit transformed, in the modern world. Walcott, of course, is a
literary epic poet, but there are also some continuing examples of
orality and epic in the post-colonial world. Stephen Belcher has
studied the African oral epic tradition in his book *Epic Traditions*

of Africa, which includes a chapter that highlights the continuing production of such epics (Belcher 1999: 164–85). Other work on contemporary epic can be found in Beissinger et al (1999), including oral and sung epic from the South Balkans and Arabia. The root of these investigations can be found in the work of Albert Bates Lord, who continued the work of Milman Parry on South Balkan epic in the 1930s. A work of literary ethnography, Lord's *The Singer of Tales* (first published in 1960) demonstrates how the performance of epic songs influenced the transition from oral to literary artefacts and he applied his ideas to the *Odyssey* and the *Iliad*, with some comments on medieval epic as well. *The Singer Resumes the Tale* (edited and published posthumously in 1995) extends the notes on the medieval material contained in the previous volume to a fuller treatment of texts such as *Beowulf*. At the same time as Lord was conducting his research, the Greek ethnographer James Notopoulos was recording and analysing modern performances of Greek epics across Greece in order to show how the techniques of the oral poet have survived.

Walcott is not, however, the only contemporary writer to engage with epic and gender. In *The Penelopiad* (2005), the Canadian post-colonial novelist, poet and critic Margaret Atwood points to the exclusion of women's experience from the epic tradition. She uses the principle of inversion to question categories that have been used to elaborate epic meanings, and she does so by giving Penelope the voice that has been denied women in epic, allowing her to comment on her own position as a valued commodity. Penelope's narrative undercuts epic masculine heroism, fate and religion, laying them open to interrogation as ideological constructs. The internal narration makes the reader complicit, replaying in an especially subtle form the narrative strategies by which the audience is made to identify with the epic project. Atwood takes this logic, which in some respects is similar to that employed in theatre by Brecht, a stage further:

> The Chorus Line:
> The Wily Captain, A Sea Shanty
> As Performed by the Twelve Maids, in Sailor Costumes
>
> (Atwood 2005: 93)

This is the heading to Chapter XIII, and provides one example whereby Atwood gives a voice to the women servants executed by Odysseus, thus introducing an alternative heteroglossic element into what was once perceived as a monolithic narrative.

Atwood is also able to inhabit the genres of both the epic and science fiction, as she shows in her novel *The Handmaid's Tale* (1985), where she imagines a dystopian future America in which the birth-rate has plummeted. This amalgamation of literary forms is something that she has in common with the fantasy and science fiction writer Ursula K. Le Guin. The latter's novel *Lavinia* (2008) refashions the *Aeneid* in order to reimagine the narrative from the perspective of Virgil's Latin princess. Both *The Penelopiad* and *Lavinia* make explicit the connection between epic and some of the late twentieth century's most popular novel forms, but it has to be said that both fantasy and science fiction have had a long history of engagement with epic elements. The boom in science fiction can also at least partly be explained by the contemporary fascination with all things technological. Series such as E.E. Doc Smith's *Lensman* and *Skylark* books and novels such as A.E. van Vogt's *Voyage of the Space Beagle* straddle the period just before and after the Second World War. They are usually described as "space opera", a designation which has obvious resonances with those operatic forms that descended from the epic, as we observed in the case of the Wagnerian reworking of the *Nibelungenlied* in Chapter 3. Other well-known science fiction novels and series often lay a more serious claim to the materials of epic, such as Frank Herbert's *Dune* books, the first in the series of which was published in 1965, to be followed by five more that sought to expand the timescale of the universe he created. These novels narrate the rise to supreme power of the noble House of the Atreides, clearly descended from the Greek hero Atreus, the father of the Homeric kings Menelaus and Agamemnon. Similarly, there are echoes of the saga form in many other science fiction series, especially those which tend to be driven by the adventures of a main character. Long-running series would include E.C. Tubb's *Dumarest* novels, the first of which, *The Winds of Gath*, was initially published in 1967. An especially well-known humorous series is Harry Harrison's *Stainless Steel*

Rat, which satirises many of the conventions of science fiction and whose main character, like many of the early novel's 'low life' characters such as Defoe's Moll Flanders, is a thief.

Even as it reworks epic elements, science fiction creates a world or universe that goes well beyond current levels of knowledge, replacing the importance of the divine that is so often associated with the epic with advanced technology. The modern prose fantasy epic enacts a similar operation although of course in this case the emphasis is on magic as opposed to science. The massive success of J.R.R. Tolkien's novels has been significant in this regard, especially his domestication of epic via the saga in *The Hobbit* and *The Lord of the Rings*. Tolkien and his academic compatriot, C.S. Lewis, began by creating children's stories in the form of *The Hobbit* and *The Chronicles of Narnia*, but Tolkien quickly capitalised on his specialist knowledge of Anglo-Saxon and the sagas to flesh out the history of the world he created in *The Lord of the Rings* as well as in many other stories. Both writers insist upon a pseudo-Christian worldview for their fantasies, rooting their invented mythologies in elements of the force of divine power that are familiar from the epic tradition. For example, Tolkien writes an entire creation scene complete with emerging Lucifer-figure in *The Silmarillion* and C.S. Lewis constructs a principle of moral order that underpins his multiple realities. Epic offers a worldview and both novelists make Christian narrative part of it, remaking Milton's Satan in their own images. Even when divested of their implicitly Christian content, their techniques, especially those of Tolkien, have influenced many subsequent writers, such as Stephen Donaldson, who has written nine Thomas Covenant books so far (the first was published in 1977), and Julian May's *Saga of the Exiles*, the first of which was published in 1982. Donaldson adds variation to the tradition he inherited from Tolkien by making his hero reluctant at best, centring the narrative on his actions in the manner of a saga, while May experiments with time travel via advanced technology, mixing fantasy and science fiction elements together.

However, this is not to say that the influence of Tolkien and Lewis has always been viewed positively. The British writer

Michael Moorcock, an extremely prolific novelist and polemicist himself, characterises their works as "Epic Pooh", reducing their novels to the level of the children's character Winnie the Pooh, in a journalistic piece that is incorporated into his work of criticism on science fiction and fantasy (Moorcock 1987: 121–39); in particular, he attacks the reactionary politics of such writers and their relatively closed, pseudo-Christian morality. Moorcock's own output is prodigious and he is perhaps the best-known exponent of fiction that explores multiple realities. This has enabled him to incorporate many of his individual fantasy characters into an overall story arc, a sort of epic of an Eternal Champion figure who is continually reincarnated as an important heroic figure in multiple realities. One of the most significant elements of these stories is their resolutely anti-moralistic stance; Moorcock invents a cosmic battle between forces of Law and Chaos in order to break out of the dichotomy of good and evil, using a great deal of epic and saga material to do so, especially in the *Elric* (saga) and *Corum* (Celtic-influenced) books. Both heroes are recognisably 'elven' in ways that are familiar from Tolkien, but Moorcock deliberately subverts what he sees as Tolkien's naïve moralising by beginning the Corum books with the eponymous hero's mutilation by humans. Elric is the sickly last Emperor of a sorcerous pre-human empire. He acquires his life energy from a vampiric black runesword that steals the life energy of those it kills and passes some of it onto its wielder. At one point, Moorcock's representation of the multiverse permits Elric to enter a fantasy version of our own world. He battles the sleeping hero Roland in order to take from him the Horn of Fate, which Elric needs to complete the renewal of his home earth (Moorcock 1983b: 157–65). This insertion of the legend of Roland into a modern fantasy novel enables the twentieth-century writer to incorporate already existing epic elements into a new epic format.

However, such echoes of epic are not restricted to literary forms. One of the most vibrant areas into which epic forms are translated is the visual medium of film, and latterly, that of television. The American film industry produced its own home-grown variants with Cecil B. DeMille's biblical films, which are usually described as epics because of their sheer scale, and they remodel Christian or Roman history as foundational narratives. There is a further line of descent running from *Metropolis* (1927) to *Blade Runner* (1982) and from DeMille to *Gladiator* (2000); both *Blade Runner* and *Gladiator* are directed by Ridley Scott, the director of *Alien* (1979). The most famous grand science fiction films that deal with 'epic' themes are probably the *Star Wars* movies, which are often described in terms of the saga because of their focus on several main characters within a larger context of empire.

It comes as no surprise to find that fragments of epic also appear in the related medium of television. Long-running series existed almost from the beginning of commercial programming, following on from a similar radio format: the soap opera, which itself borrowed from the novel and theatre. Following on from the comments made in Chapter 1 in relation to the long nineteenth-century novels such as those by Dickens or Tolstoy (many of which first appeared in serialised form), it is possible to see how novelistic family 'sagas' infiltrate the new visual media. It does not take a great leap of imagination to marry the format with the science fiction or fantasy genre to create another variation; for example the *Journey Into Space* series that was so popular on BBC radio in the 1950s was an extension of this kind of fusion of genres. Probably the most famous of the television series that followed was *Star Trek*, which shared a great deal with A.E. van Vogt's premise for the Space Beagle; the importance for each of the exploration of space was a very contemporary topic for the 1960s, and already had access to a handy set of references in pre-existing science fiction literature. The application of the term 'saga' to *Star Trek* is rather misleading, because the series (and its subsequent film franchise) did not really have a coherent overall storyline. It was more a series of disparate single episodes, connected by the continuing focus on a small group of main characters, although individual films have a much clearer focus in the ways that they deal with contemporary political and cultural issues. The various successor series do tend to have more continuity in their utilisation of a stable fictional universe.

The creator of *Babylon 5*, J. Michael Straczynski, learned from *Star Trek* and provided his series with much more of a linear overall plotline. The series has sub-plots, of course, and also generates its own sequels and spin-offs, but the overall sense of direction gives it a different kind of coherence from its competitors, lending it much more of the feel of an 'epic' linear narrative as it moves through a range of pre-planned major events. It is also an extremely literate production, making references to Moorcock's *Elric* as well as to Tolkien, among others, and so the programme modulates epic elements through previously existing fantasy literature that is itself derived from epic. This may partly be due to the influence of the American science fiction writer Harlan Ellison, who is credited as creative consultant to the show. One of the most impressive *coups* achieved by this series is its casting of Walter Koenig, who played the young, impetuous and idealistic Chekov in *Star Trek,* as the ruthless fascistic psi-cop Bester. There is also an example of multiple referentiality here, since the *Babylon 5* character is named after the science fiction writer Alfred Bester. Post-modern multimedia reference is rarely so complex, although comparisons could also be made with Christopher Nolan's recent *Dark Knight* trilogy of Batman films.

CONTEMPORARY

The twentieth century has moved us a long way from the first epics, with visual media such as film and television providing the most accessible and easily recognised forms of epic influence. In addition to science fiction series, there are the fantasy equivalents such as *Xena*, *Hercules* and *Spartacus: Blood and Sand,* and recent urban/gothic adaptations (*Buffy*, *Angel* and the *Twilight* franchise). Particularly with *Twilight*, it becomes difficult to disentangle which medium is influencing which: does the literature come first, or is it then influenced in turn by the series? Or by film? In terms of the relationship with epic, what matters are the ways in which an oral form with a long literary history fractures along very specific lines. Its components then feed into new genres and forms, and ultimately into media that were unthinkable to the first audiences of *Gilgamesh*.

In strictly generic terms, multimedia fictions could never be counted as epic forms in their own right, although they do provide something of a return to the communal aspect of epic. This can be seen in the multiplicity of very contemporary formats that are becoming available to a much wider cross-section of society than ever before. The exponential growth of the computer games industry has included science fiction sagas such as the *Wing Commander Series*; it now includes the online *World of Warcraft* and the various worlds of the *Sims*. *Wing Commander* has a relatively constrained plotline, with some variations determined by player actions, while *Warcraft* provides the parameters within which the players operate. *The Sims* is almost free-form, in the best traditions of analogue role-playing games such as *Dungeons & Dragons*; preceding the rise of the computer games industry, it is possible to discern a type of modern medievalism in the worldview and rules of the latter. Derived from the fiction of fantasy writers such as Tolkien, fantasy role-playing games such as *Dungeons & Dragons* should be distinguished from the nineteenth-century medievalism of writers such as Tennyson and Browning because the form of the game can be so easily adapted to other genres such as science fiction and horror.

The more open-ended role-playing games permit a group of players, whether online or in small gatherings, to co-operate in the creation of their own 'epic' productions. They can be epic in various ways: the communal or group requirements for this activity are crucial and the continuing story focuses on a small number of main characters over many playing sessions, lending the game great scope. What matters is the acquisition of creative potential by and for individuals and groups, a peculiar and appropriately post-modern return to the conditions of epic performance. It is tellingly symptomatic that the first edition of the 'hard' science fiction role-playing game *Traveller* features as its blurb a distress call from a spaceship named the *Beowulf* (Miller 1977). Here the game designer Marc Miller returns to *Beowulf,* albeit for different reasons from those of Albert Bates Lord. Epic elements inform contemporary developments in post-modern genres of all kinds. This might seem to indicate that epic in and of itself is no longer possible, but the survival of some of the main elements of oral epic into the twentieth century and beyond demonstrates that any attempt to write the genre's epitaph would be premature. Throughout its long history, epic has shown a remarkable propensity to transformation and adaptation that sometimes exceeds the desires of its practitioners. Clearly the history of epic is far from complete.

Glossary

Akkad – the area now known as Northern Iraq. Akkadian invaders conquered the Sumerian civilisation to their south, establishing the first known empire.

Allegory – a literary technique that uses familiar language to convey a far deeper spiritual and moral meaning.

Apotheosis – a Greek term meaning the attainment of godhood.

Babylon – a major city-state in Southern Mesopotamia that became the centre of a major empire after the collapse of the earlier Akkadian state.

Brythonic Celts – the Celtic inhabitants of the areas now known as Wales, Cornwall and Brittany. There are some cultural and linguistic differences between these and the Celts of Ireland and what is now Scotland.

Consuls – the two annually elected magistrates at the apex of the Roman Republic's political system.

Cuneiform – an early form of writing composed of geometrical patterns inscribed onto mud tablets that were then baked to ensure permanence.

Epithet – descriptive term or short phrase.

Ethos – a set of overall beliefs.

Expressionism – an artistic movement that emerged in early twentieth-century Germany that stressed the importance of the individual viewpoint.

Extended simile – a comparison of such length that it temporarily becomes a major textual feature in its own right.

Genre – literary classification.

Humanism – the cultivation of a set of values derived in part from the redistribution of the Latin and Greek classics in Europe; an important guiding influence of the Renaissance.

Ideology – the world view that underpins the political actions and structures of a social group.

Imperium – originally, the assumption of military authority by a Roman magistrate. More widely, it refers to the imperial state, an empire that subsumes other states into itself, usually by military conquest.

Intertextuality – the process by which a literary work makes references to other texts a major part of its own meanings.

Mesopotamia – the area between the rivers Tigris and Euphrates.

Middle Ages – conventionally in Europe, the period between roughly the fall of the Western Roman Empire and the Renaissance. The term 'Dark Ages' is no longer used for the early part of this period.

Mock heroic – poems that use the conventions of the epic to make fun of it.

Modernism – a literary movement beginning in the late nineteenth century that reacted against traditional styles and techniques.

Motif – a narrative element that appears more than once.

Mycenaeans – the inhabitants of Greece at the time of the Trojan War.

Paradigm – overarching model.

Patriarchy – a social system that privileges men over women.

Pentateuch – the first five books of the Bible as they are known in the Christian tradition.

Persia – in ancient times, this term refers to the area under the control of the Emperor of the Medes and Persians, who thought of themselves as a grouping of Iranians. The modern state of Iran changed its name so as to differentiate itself from the Persia of the Shah as a means to stress its own cultural identity. The two are in practice used interchangeably by historians.

Picaresque – term often applied to novels of the seventeenth century that depict the society of rogues and scoundrels.

Post-colonialism – a literary movement that seeks to engage with, critique and move beyond the cultural monolith of empire.

Principate – the monarchical system established by Augustus to run the Roman Empire.

Reformation – the movement within early Renaissance Christianity that led to the formation of various kinds of Protestantism.

Renaissance – a period of about 250 years from the early fifteenth century onwards in Europe that saw the flowering of classical models of influence on all areas of the arts, beginning in Italy and moving outwards. Different countries experienced their own Renaissance at different times.

Romance – subset of epic descended from the *Odyssey* and especially popular in Western Europe from about the thirteenth century onwards.

Romulus – mythical founder of the City of Rome.

Saga – Norse and Icelandic prose narratives about the pagan past written in Christian times.

Sanskrit – one of the oldest members of the Indo-European family of languages.

Satire – humour with an edge, used to attack various moral and political targets.

Sumer – possibly the earliest civilisation, Sumer was comprised of a number of individual city-states. They flourished in the fourth millennium BCE in the area now known as Southern Iraq.

Svarga – Sanskrit term meaning ritual sacrifice.

Tora – the first five books of the Hebrew Bible.

Triumvirate – loose alliance of convenience between three men who divide up the late Roman Republic amongst themselves.

Trope – an element of figurative language.

Typology – a systematic process of classification.

Zoroastrianism – monotheistic Persian religion.

BIBLIOGRAPHY

PRIMARY READING

ANCIENT AND CLASSICAL EPIC

Apollonius of Rhodes: *Jason and the Golden Fleece* ed. Richard Hunter (Oxford: Oxford University Press, World's Classics edition, 2009).

Aristotle: 'On the Art of Poetry' in T.S. Dorsch trans.: *Aristotle, Horace, Longinus: Classical Literary Criticism* (Harmondsworth: Penguin Books, 1985), 31–75.

The Bible Authorised King James Version (Glasgow: Collins, 1839).

Caesar: *The Conquest of Gaul* trans. Jane Gardner and S. Handford (London: Penguin Classics, 2003).

Dalley, Stephanie ed.: *Myths From Mesopotamia: Creation, The Flood, Gilgamesh and Others* (Oxford: Oxford University Press, revised edition 2008).

Davies, M. ed.: *Epicorum Graecorum Fragmenta* (Gottingen, 1988).

Ennius: *Annales* in *Remains of Old Latin, Vol. 1* (Loeb Classical Library, revised edition 1989).

Euripides: *Medea and Other Plays* ed. Philip Vellacott (London: Penguin, 2002).

Flaccus, Valerius: *Argonautica* trans. J.H. Mozley (London and Cambridge, MA: Harvard University Press, 1936).

Hesiod: *Theogony and Works and Days* ed. M.L. West (Oxford: Oxford University Press, 1988).

Homer: *The Iliad* ed. Martin Hammond (London: Penguin Books, 1987).

Homer: *The Odyssey* trans. Robert Fagles (New York: Penguin Books, 1996).

Italicus, Silius: *Punica* (Loeb Classical Library 2 vols, 1989).

James, Alan ed.: *The Trojan Epic: Posthomerica* (Baltimore: Johns Hopkins University Press, 2007).

Lucan: *Pharsalia* trans. Edward Ridley (Middlesex: The Echo Library, 2008).

Lucretius: *The Nature of Things* trans. A.E. Stallings (London: Penguin Books, 2007).

Naevius: *Bellum Poenicum* in *Remains of Old Latin, Vol. 2* (Loeb Classical Library, revised edition 1989).

Nonnos: *Dionysiaca* (Loeb Classical Library 3 vols, 1989).

Ovid: *Metamorphoses* trans. Arthur Golding, ed. Madeleine Forey (London: Penguin Books, 2002).

Pliny: *The Letters of the Younger Pliny* trans. Betty Radice (London and New York: Penguin Books, 1968).

Smith, John D. ed.: *The Mahabharata* (London: Penguin Books, 2009).

Statius, Publius Papinius: *The Thebaid: Seven Against Thebes* ed. Charles Stanley Ross (Baltimore: Johns Hopkins University Press, 2004).

Valmiki: *The Ramayana* trans. Arshia Sattar (New Delhi: Penguin Books India, 2000).

Virgil: *The Aeneid* ed. C. Day Lewis (Oxford: Oxford University Press, reprinted 2008).

FROM THE HEROIC TOWARDS ROMANCE AND ALLEGORY

Aneirin: *The Gododdin* trans. Steve Short (Felinfach: Llanerch Publishers, 1994).

Burgess, Glyn S. ed.: *The Song of Roland* (London and New York: Penguin Books, 1990).

Byock, Jesse L. ed.: *The Saga of the Volsungs* (London and New York: Penguin Books, 1990).

Chaucer, Geoffrey: *The Canterbury Tales* trans. Nevill Coghill (London and New York: Penguin Books, 2003).

Cook, Robert ed.: *Njal's Saga* (London and New York: Penguin Books, 2001).

Dante: *Dante's Divine Comedy: Hell, Purgatory, Paradise* trans. Henry W. Longfellow (London: Arcturus Publishing, 2010).

Donoghue, Daniel ed.: *Beowulf: A Verse Translation* trans. Seamus Heaney (New York and London: W.W. Norton, 2002).

Edwards, Cyril ed.: *The Nibelungenlied: The Lay of the Nibelungs* (Oxford: Oxford University Press, 2010).

Fardusi: *The Shah-Namah of Fardusi* trans. Alexander Rogers (Delhi: D.K. Publishers, 1995).

France, Marie de: *The Lais of Marie de France* eds. Glyn S. Burgess and Keith Busby (London and New York: Penguin Books, 2003).

Gantz, Jeffrey ed. and trans.: *The Mabinogion* (London and New York: Penguin Books, 1976).

Gantz, Jeffrey ed.: *Early Irish Myths and Sagas* (London and New York: Penguin Books, 1981).

Griffiths, Bill ed.: *The Battle of Maldon: Text and Translation* (Norfolk: Anglo-Saxon Books, 2000).

Jones, Gwyn ed.: *Erik the Red and Other Icelandic Sagas* (Oxford: Oxford University Press, 2008).

Kellogg, Robert: 'Introduction' in *The Sagas of Icelanders* various trans. (London and New York: Penguin Books, 2001).

Monmouth, Geoffrey of: *The History of the Kings of Britain* trans. Neil Wright (Woodbridge: The Boydell Press, 2007).

Newth, Michael: *Heroes of the French Epic: Translations from the Chansons de Geste* (Suffolk and New York: The Boydell Press, 2005).

Oskarsdottir, Svanhildur ed.: *Egil's Saga* trans. Bernard Scudder (London and New York: Penguin Books, 2004).

Palsson, Hermann and Edwards, Paul eds.: *Orkneyinga Saga: The History of the Earls of Orkney* (London and New York: Penguin Books, 1981).

Treharne, Elaine ed.: *Old & Middle English c.890–c.1450: An Anthology* 3rd edition (Chichester: Wiley-Blackwell, 2010).

Troyes, Chrétien de: *Arthurian Romances* ed. William W. Kibler (London and New York: Penguin Books, 2004).

THE RENAISSANCE AND THE EARLY NOVEL

Ariosto, Ludovico: *Orlando Furioso* trans. Guido Waldman (Oxford: Oxford University Press, 2008).

Beaumont, Francis: *The Knight of the Burning Pestle* ed. Andrew Gurr (Edinburgh: Oliver & Boyd, 1968).

Behn, Aphra: *Oroonoko* ed. Janet Todd (London and New York: Penguin Books, 2003).

Boiardo, Matteo Maria: *Orlando Innamorato* trans. Charles Stanley Ross (Oxford and New York: Oxford University Press, 1995).

Camoes, Luis Vaz de: *The Lusiads* trans. Landeg White (Oxford: Oxford University Press, 2008).

Cervantes, Miguel de: *Don Quixote* trans. John Rutherford (London and New York: Penguin Books, 2003).

Malory, Sir Thomas: *Le Morte d'Arthur* ed. Stephen H.A. Shephard (New York and London: W.W. Norton, 2004).

Milton, John: *Paradise Lost* ed. Christopher Ricks (Harmondsworth: Penguin Books, 1968).

Milton, John: *Poetical Works* ed. Douglas Bush (Oxford and New York: Oxford University Press, 1990).

Rabelais, François: *Gargantua and Pantagruel* trans. M.A. Screech (London and New York: Penguin Books, 2006).

Sidney, Philip: *The Old Arcadia* ed. Katharine Duncan-Jones (Oxford: Oxford University Press, 2008).

Spenser, Edmund: *The Faerie Queene* ed. Thomas P. Roche Jr. (Harmondsworth: Penguin Books, 1984).

Tasso, Torquato: *The Liberation of Jerusalem* trans. Max Wickert (Oxford: Oxford University Press, 2009).

EPIC IN THE AGE OF THE INDIVIDUAL

Arneson, Dave and Gygax, Gary: *Dungeons & Dragons* (Wisconsin: TSR, 1974).

Atwood, Margaret: *The Penelopiad* (Edinburgh: Canongate Books, 2005).

Barlow, Joel: *The Columbiad: A Poem* (Michigan: University of Michigan Library Scholarly Publishing Office, 2006).

Blake, William: *William Blake: The Complete Poems* ed. Alicia Ostriker (Harmondsworth: Penguin Books, 1983).

Brecht, Bertolt: *Brecht On Theatre: The Development of an Aesthetic* ed. and trans. John Willett (London: Methuen, 1978).

Brecht, Bertolt: *Mother Courage and Her Children* trans. John Willett (London: Methuen, 1980).

Butler, Samuel: *Hudibras* (Gloucester: Dodo Press, 2005).

Byron, George Gordon: *The Oxford Authors: Byron* ed. Jerome J. McGann (Oxford and New York: Oxford University Press, 1991).

Coleridge, Samuel Taylor: *Coleridge's Notebooks: A Selection* ed. Seamus Perry (Oxford: Oxford University Press, 2002).

Defoe, Daniel: *Moll Flanders* (London and New York: Penguin Books, 2003).

Donaldson, Stephen: *Lord Foul's Bane* (Glasgow: Fontana Books, 1978).

Dostoevsky, Fyodor: *The Brothers Karamazov* trans. David McDuff (London and New York: Penguin Books, 2003).

Dostoevsky, Fyodor: *Crime and Punishment* ed. Richard Peace, trans. Jessie Coulson (Oxford: Oxford University Press, 2008).

Dryden, John: *The Major Works* (Oxford: Oxford University Press, 2003).

Eliot, T.S.: *Collected Poems 1909–1962* (London: Faber & Faber, 1974).

Fielding, Henry: *Tom Jones* ed. R.P.C. Mutter (London and New York: Penguin Books, 1985).

Fielding, Henry: *Joseph Andrews and Shamela* (Oxford: Oxford Paperbacks, 2008).

Harrison, Harry: *The Stainless Steel Rat Omnibus* (London: Gollancz, 2008).

Herbert, Frank: *Dune* (London: Hodder, 1982).

Howard, Robert E: *The Complete Chronicles of Conan Centenary Edition* (London: Gollancz, 2006).

Joyce, James: *Ulysses* (Harmondsworth: Penguin Books, 1985).

Kazantzakis, Nikos: *The Odyssey: A Modern Sequel* trans. Kimon Friar (New York: Simon & Schuster, 1958).

Keats, John: *John Keats: The Complete Poems* ed. John Barnard (Harmondsworth: Penguin Books, 1983).

Lewis, C.S.: *The Complete Chronicles of Narnia* (New York and Glasgow: Harper-Collins Children's Books, 2001).

Lonnrot, Elias: *The Kalevala* trans. Keith Bosley (Oxford: Oxford University Press, 2008).

Macpherson, James: *The Poems of Ossian* (Forgotten Books, 2007).

May, Julian: *The Many-Coloured Land* (New York: Tor Books, 1982).

Moorcock, Michael: *The Chronicles of Corum* (New York: Berkley Publishing Group, 1983a).

Moorcock, Michael: *Stormbringer* (London: Granada, 1983b)

Moorcock, Michael: *Elric of Melnibone* (London: Gollancz, 2001).

Perren, Jeff and Gygax, Gary: *Chainmail* (Wisconsin: TSR, 1971).

Pope, Alexander: *Pope: Poetical Works* ed. Herbert Davis (Oxford and New York: Oxford University Press, 1983).

Pullman, Philip: *His Dark Materials Trilogy: Northern Lights, Subtle Knife, Amber Spyglass* (New York: Scholastic, 2008).

Richardson, Samuel: *Pamela: Or Virtue Rewarded* (Oxford: Oxford Paperbacks, 2008).

Shelley, Mary: *Frankenstein, or The Modern Prometheus* (Hertfordshire: Wordsworth Editions Ltd, 1994).

Shelley, Percy Bysshe: *The Major Works* eds. Zachary Leader and Michael O'Neill (Oxford: Oxford University Press, 2009).

Smith, E.E. 'Doc': *The Lensman Series* (New York and Glasgow: Panther Books, 1980).

Smith, E.E. 'Doc': *The Skylark of Space* (Rockville, MD: Wildside Press, 2007).

Southey, Robert: *Joan of Arc* (Whitefish, MT: Kessinger Publishing, 2005).

Sterne, Laurence: *The Life and Opinions of Tristram Shandy* ed. Ian Campbell Ross (Oxford and New York: Oxford University Press, 1983).

Sterne, Laurence: *A Sentimental Journey* (London and New York: Penguin Books, 2005).

Strindberg, August: *Plays, Vol. 1* trans. Michael Meyer (London: Secker & Warburg, 1964).

Swift, Jonathan: *Gulliver's Travels* (London and New York: Penguin Books, 2003).

Tennyson, Alfred Lord: *The Works of Alfred Lord Tennyson* (Hertfordshire: Wordsworth Editions Limited, 2008).

Tolkien, J.R.R.: *The Hobbit: 70th Anniversary Edition* (New York and Glasgow: HarperCollins, 1993).

Tolkien, J.R.R.: *The Lord of the Rings* (New York and Glasgow: HarperCollins, 2007).

Tolstoy, Leo: *Anna Karenina* trans. Richard Pevear and Larissa Volokhonsky (London and New York: Penguin Books, 2003).

Tolstoy, Leo: *War and Peace* trans. Anthony Briggs (London and New York: Penguin Books, 2007).

Tubb, E.C.: *The Winds of Gath* (London: Arrow Books, 1972).

van Vogt, A.E.: *The Voyage of the Space Beagle* (London and New York: Orb Books, 2008).

Walcott, Derek: *Omeros* (London: Faber & Faber, 1990).

Wordsworth, William: *The Collected Poems of William Wordsworth* (London: Wordsworth Editions Limited, 2006).

SECONDARY READING

ANCIENT AND CLASSICAL EPIC

Armstrong, Richard Hamilton: 'Translating Ancient Epic' in Foley ed. (2009), 174–95.

Barnes, Michael H.: 'Claudian' in Foley ed. (2009), 538–49.

Bartsch, Shadi: 'Lucan' in Foley ed. (2009): 492–502.

Brockington, John: *The Sanskrit Epics* (London, Boston and Cologne: Brill, 1998).

Burgess, Jonathan S.: 'The Epic Cycle and Fragments' in Foley ed. (2009), 344–52.

Burkert, Walter: 'Near Eastern Connections' in Foley ed. (2009), 291–301.

Dalley, Stephanie, Reyes, A.T., Pingree, David, Salvesen, Alison, and McCall, Henrietta: *The Legacy of Mesopotamia* (Oxford: Oxford University Press, 1998).

Davidson, Olga M: 'Persian/Iranian Epic' in Foley ed. (2009), 264–76.

Dominik, William J.: 'Statius' in Foley ed. (2009), 514–27.

Dorson, Richard M.: 'Introduction' in Oinas ed. (1977), 1–7.

Foley, John Miles ed.: *A Companion to Ancient Epic* (Malden, MA and Oxford: Wiley-Blackwell, 2009).

George, A.R.: 'The Epic of *Gilgamesh*' in Bates ed. (2010), 1–12.

Goldberg, Susan M.: 'Early Republican Epic' in Foley ed. (2009), 429–39.

Griffin, Jasper: 'Introduction' in Virgil (2008), ix–xiv.

Jenkyns, Richard: 'Introduction'in Lucretius (2007), vii–xxiii.

Katz, Joshua T.: 'The Indo-European Context' in Foley ed. (2009), 20–30.

Knox, Bernard: 'Introduction' in Homer (1996), 3–64.

Martin, Richard P.: 'Epic as Genre' in Foley ed. (2009), 9–19.

Mozley, D.H.: 'Introduction' in Flaccus (1936).

Nelis, D.P.: 'Apollonius of Rhodes' in Foley ed. (2009), 353–63.

Nelson, Stephanie: 'Hesiod' in Foley ed. (2009), 330–43.

Newlands, Carole E.: 'Ovid' in Foley ed. (2009), 476–91.

Niditch, Susan: 'The Challenge of Israelite Epic' in Foley ed. (2009), 277–88.

Parry, Milman: *The Making of Homeric Verse: The Collected Papers of Milman Parry* ed. A. Parry (Oxford: Oxford University Press, new edition 1988).

Sasson, Jack M.: 'Comparative Observations on the Near Eastern Epic Traditions' in Foley ed. (2009), 215–32.

Sattar, Arshia: 'Translator's Note' in Valmiki (2000a), i–xvi.

Sattar, Arshia: 'Introduction' in Valmiki (2000b), xvii–lviii.

Zissos, Andrew: 'Valerius Flaccus' in Foley ed. (2009), 503–13.

FROM THE HEROIC TOWARDS ROMANCE AND ALLEGORY

Chance, Jane: 'The Structural Unity of *Beowulf*: The Problem of Grendel's Mother' in Donoghue ed. (2002), 152–67.

Elias, Norbert: *The Court Society* trans. Edmund Jephcott (Oxford: Blackwell, 1983).

Frank, Roberta: 'The *Beowulf* Poet's Sense of History' in Donoghue ed. (2002): 167–81.

Gejin, Chao: 'Mongolian Oral Epic Poetry: An Overview' in *Oral Tradition* 12/2 (1997), http://journal.oraltradition.org/files/articles/12ii/5_gejin.pdf.

Heaney, Seamus: 'Translator's Introduction' in Donoghue ed. (2002), xxiii–xxxviii.

Helgason, Jon Karl: 'Continuity? The Icelandic Sagas in Post-Medieval Times' in McTurk ed. (2007), 64–81.

Hill, Thomas D.: 'The Christian Language and Theme of *Beowulf*' in Donoghue ed. (2002), 197–211.

Kallendorf, Craig: 'Virgil's Post-classical Legacy' in Foley ed. (2009), 574–88.

Laxness, Halldór: *Islandsklukkan* (Reykjavik, 1943).

Laxness, Halldór: *Iceland's Bell* trans. Philip Roughton (New York: Vintage, 2003).

Lewis, C.S.: *The Allegory of Love* (London: Oxford University Press, 1938).

Leyerle, John: 'The Interlace Structure of *Beowulf*' in Donoghue ed. (2002), 130–52.

McTurk, Rory ed.: *A Companion to Old Norse-Icelandic Literature and Culture* (Malden, MA, Oxford and Carlton: Blackwell, 2007).

Olason, Vesteinn: 'Family Sagas' in McTurk ed. (2007), 101–18.

Robinson, Fred C.: 'The Tomb of Beowulf' in Donoghue ed. (2002), 181–97.

Tulinius, Torfi H.: 'Sagas of Icelandic Prehistory' in McTurk ed. (2007), 447–61.

THE RENAISSANCE AND THE EARLY NOVEL

Bakhtin, Mikhail Mikhailovich: *Rabelais and His World* trans. Helene Iswolsky (Bloomington: Indiana University Press, 1984).

Empson, William: *Milton's God* (Cambridge: Cambridge University Press, 1981).

Greenblatt, Stephen J.: *Renaissance Self-Fashioning: From More to Shakespeare* (Chicago: The University of Chicago Press, 1984).

Mazotta, Giuseppe: 'Italian Renaissance Epic' in Bates ed. (2010), 93–118.

Sinfield, Alan: *Faultlines: Cultural Materialism and the Politics of Dissident Reading* (Oxford: Clarendon Press, 1992).

Watt, Ian: *The Rise of the Novel* (Harmondsworth: Penguin Books, 1963).

EPIC IN THE AGE OF THE INDIVIDUAL

Beissinger, Margaret, Tylus, Jane, and Wofford, Suzanne eds.: *Epic Traditions in the Contemporary World: The Poetics of Community* (California: University of California Press, 1999).

Belcher, Stephen: *Epic Traditions of Africa* (Bloomington: Indiana University Press, 1999).

Childs, Peter: *Modernism* (Abingdon: Routledge, 2008).

Hamner, Robert D.: *Epic of the Dispossessed: Derek Walcott's Omeros* (Columbia and London: University of Missouri Press, 1997).

Lefevere, Andre: 'The Gates of Analogy: The *Kalevala* in English' in Susan Bassnett and Andre Lefevere: *Constructing Cultures: Essays on Literary Translation* (Cleveden: Multilingual Matters Ltd, 1998), 76–89.

Lukacs, Georg: *The Historical Novel* (London: Merlin Press Limited, 1983).

Spender, Dale: *Mothers of the Novel: 100 Good Women Novelists Before Jane Austen* (Norfolk: Pandora Books, 1986).

GENERAL READING

Bakhtin, Mikhail Mikhailovich: *The Dialogic Imagination: Four Essays by M.M. Bakhtin* ed. Michael Holquist (Austin: University of Texas Press, 1975).

Bates, Catherine ed.: *The Cambridge Companion to the Epic* (Cambridge: Cambridge University Press, 2010).

Bloom, Harold: *The Anxiety of Influence* (Oxford: Oxford University Press, 1997).

Coupe, Laurence: *Myth* 2nd edition (Abingdon: Routledge, 2009).

Danow, David K.: *The Thought of Mikhail Bakhtin: From Word to Culture* (New York: St Martin's Press, 1991).

de Groot, Jerome: *The Historical Novel* (London and New York: Routledge, 2010).

Genette, Gerard: *The Architext* trans. Robert Scholes (Berkeley: University of California Press, 1992).

Goody, Jack: *The Interface Between the Written and the Oral* (Cambridge: Cambridge University Press, 1993).

Holquist, Michael: *Dialogism: Bakhtin and His World* (London: Routledge, 1991).

Lévi-Strauss, Claude: *Structural Anthropology* (Harmondsworth: Penguin, 1968).

Lévi-Strauss, Claude: *Myth and Meaning* (London: Routledge, 1978).

Lord, Albert Bates: *Singer of Tales* (London: Macmillan, 1965).

Lord, Albert Bates: *The Singer Resumes the Tale* ed. Mary Louise Lord (Ithaca and London: Cornell University Press, 1995).

Manguel, Alberto: *Homer's The Iliad and The Odyssey: A Biography* (London: Atlantic Books, 2007).

Miller, Marc: *Traveller* (Illinois: Game Designer's Workshop, 1977).

Moorcock, Michael: *Wizardry and Wild Romance* (London: Victor Gollancz, 1987).

Oinas, Felix J. ed.: *Heroic Epic and Saga: An Introduction to the World's Great Folk Epics* (Bloomington and London: Indiana University Press, 1978).

Quint, David: *Epic and Empire: Politics and Generic Form from Virgil to Milton* (New Jersey: Princeton University Press, 1993).

INDEX

Italicised page numbers refer to tables.